The Conservative Rebellion

Other works of interest from St. Augustine's Press

George J. Marlin, *Christian Persecutions in the Middle East: A 21st Century Tragedy*

Rémi Brague, *On the God of the Christians (and on one or two others)*

Rémi Brague, *Eccentric Culture: A Theory of Western Civilization*

Edward Feser, *The Last Superstition: A Reflection on the New Atheism*

Ernest Fortin, A.A., *Christianity and Philosophical Culture in the Fifth Century*

H.S. Gerdil, *The Anti-Emile: Reflections on the Theory and Practice of Education against the Principles of Rousseau*

Paul M. Weyrich and William S. Lind, *The Next Conservitism*

Leszek Kolakowski, *Religion: If There Is No God . . .*

C.S. Lewis and Don Giovanni Calabria, *The Latin Letters of C.S. Lewis*

Gerhart Niemeyer, *The Loss and Recovery of Truth*

Gerhart Niemeyer, *Between Nothingness and Paradise*

Gabriel Marcel, *Man against Mass Society*

Josef Pieper, *The Christian Idea of Man*

Josef Pieper, *Happiness and Contemplation*

Josef Pieper, *In Tune with the World: A Theory of Festivity*

Albert Camus, *Christian Metaphysics and Neoplatonism*

Karol Wojtyła [John Paul II], *Man in the Field of Responsibility*

Marc D. Guerra, *Liberating Logos: Pope Benedict XVI's September Speeches*

James V. Schall, *The Regensburg Lecture*

James V. Schall, *The Modern Age*

Dietrich von Hildebrand, *The Heart*

J. David Woodard, *The Politics of Morality*

Daniel J. Mahoney, *The Other Solzhenitsyn: Telling the Truth about a Misunderstood Writer and Thinker*

Helen M. Alvaré, ed., *The Conscience of the Institution*

The Conservative Rebellion

RICHARD BISHIRJIAN

ST. AUGUSTINE'S PRESS
South Bend, Indiana

Manufactured in the United States of America.

1 2 3 4 5 6   20 19 18 17 16 15

Library of Congress Cataloging in Publication Data
Bishirjian, Richard J.
The conservative rebellion / Richard Bishirjian.
pages cm
Includes index.
ISBN 978-1-58731-158-1 (hardback: alk. paper)
1. Conservatism – United States – History. 2. Decentralization in government – United States – History. 3. Liberalism – United States – History. 4. Right and left (Political science) – United States – History. I. Title.
JC573.2.U6B535 2015
320.520973 – dc23   2015005658

∞ The paper used in this publication meets the minimum requirements of the American National Standard for Information Sciences - Permanence of Paper for Printed Materials, ANSI Z39.48-1984.

ST. AUGUSTINE'S PRESS
www.staugustine.net

To Mary Theresa

Contents

Acknowledgments

I am indebted to the advice of the following colleagues who graciously read chapters from *The Conservative Rebellion*: The Honorable Tom Pauken, Dr. William Miller, Dr. Paul Gottfried, and Dr. Donald Devine. Dr. Robert Young, editor of Modern Age, tirelessly edited a chapter that is greatly improved as a result and Dr. Michael Henry applied his significant editorial skills to improvement of three chapters.

A brief glance at the contents page of *The Conservative Rebellion* will reveal an enormous debt that I owe to the Intercollegiate Studies Institute and *Modern Age*, a journal founded by Russell Kirk, and published by ISI.

"Wilson, Croly and the American Civil Religion," *Modern Age* (Winter, 1979).

"The Creation of a Conservative Intellectual: 1960–65," *Modern Age* (Winter, 1998).

"Origins and End of the New World Order," *Modern Age* (Summer, 2004).

"Leo Strauss and the American Political Religion," *Modern Age* (Fall, 2014)

Chapter 3, "Home," contains portions of chapter 11, "The Recovery of Classical-Christian Political Theory" in *The Development of Political Theory: A Critical Analysis* (Dallas: The Society for the Study of Traditional Culture, 1978).

Portions of chapter 4, "Living the Rebellion," were published in Chapter 10, "Apocalypse, History and Politics" in *The Development of Political Theory*.

Between the publication of the first essay in *Modern Age* in 1979 and sometime in 1992, I saw the outline of a book that interpreted American history in terms of distinct changes that had the look and feel of paradigms. I gave the name "the Fifth Paradigm" to a book proposal and submitted it to the Earhart Foundation. At the time I submitted that proposal, I could not have anticipated the revival of fourth paradigm Wilsonian idealism in the Presidential Administrations of two Republican Presidents, George H.W. Bush and George W. Bush. *The Conservative Rebellion* might not have been written but for the failed policies of these two American presidents.

I must thank the Earhart Foundation for its patience during the years that this was a work in progress and for its generosity.

Chapter 1
The Conservative Rebellion

Conservatives engage in rebellions, not revolutions.

The history of rebellion in America begins at Lexington and Concord. Though the disorders brought upon the English colonies by the Stamp Act and other measures were not "pogroms," nor totalitarian attempts to destroy the American colonists,[1] Americans could smell oppression and that engendered a shot "heard round the world."[2] The continuation of that tradition of rebellion in America took form in the 20th Century in the conservative "movement." That modern rebellion has been given expression in such books as *Street Corner Conservative*[3] by Bill Gavin, and even by the likes of the young Gary Wills, who recorded his remembrances of induction onto the staff of *National Review*[4] at a time when the conservative revolt began to attract opportunists—surely a sign that we conservatives were on to something.[5]

In making this argument I treat the Conservative Rebellion as an aspect of Americas self-interpretation in that aspect of our history which I call, with some optimism, its period of "recovery." As such, the social development of the Conservative Rebellion is

1   Totalitarianism would appear in France, not America, in 1789.
2   Ralph Waldo Emerson, Concord Hymn (http://www.poetryfoundation. org/poem/175140)
3   Crown Publishing, 1975.
4   Gary Wills, *Confessions of a Conservative* (New York: Doubleday, 1979).
5   Historian Walter McDougall writes of his attraction to "truth tellers." The ones he cites are rebels. "Defending America in an Age of Hustlers, Heist, and Unnecessary Wars: An Afterword," Humanitas, Vol. XXIII, Nos. 1 & 2, pp. 36–41.

what Eric Voegelin, quoting Fortescue, called an "eruption"[6] of the American spirit and mind, a paradigmatic breaking out of the American soul itself, that has been developing since the New Deal and which threatens to replace the Wilsonian political religion that dominated America in the twentieth century and, now, the twenty-first century.

The purpose of this study is to examine how, over time, the American people have come to understand their nationhood as the mystical substance of their common existence. How this paradigmatic reality of the life of a nation is articulated shapes the American nation for action in history. As such, this is a work of political theory by which its author affirms a reality that "is" at the same time that he and his fellow Conservative Rebels are its representatives. Actualizing the truth of which we are representatives is the essence of paradigmatic statesmanship.

Looking at America in this manner reveals that there have been four paradigms or, following Voegelin, "articulations of the realm," that shaped the American body politic. Not all were salutary.

The first paradigm shaped our beginning and was embodied in the "Spirit of '76." That spirit was articulated in a common Declaration of Independence of the United States that symbolized our rebellion, and the experience leading up to the momentous decision to separate the American colonies from the English crown. Today we political theorists are engaged in a heated discussion about the meaning of that symbolization. Many have interpreted the Declaration incorrectly and unleashed claims that the symbol of equality in the Declaration means equality of condition. Thomas Jefferson's choice of the words "unalienable Rights," some argue, grants the right of individuals to do what, in our hearts and minds we know, is not right. The success of the rebellion, after eight long years, and the struggle to form an effective

---

6   See Eric Voegelin's discussion of Fortescue, *The New Science of Politics. An Introduction* (Chicago: University of Chicago Press, 1952), p. 42. "A politically inarticulate social state breaks out into the articulation of the realm."

national government under the Articles of Confederation, put the contentious claims of equality and "unalienable Rights" on hold while the individual states organized themselves for governance.

The Founding of the Constitution of the United States at the Philadelphia Convention of 1787, and the articulation of the philosophy of limited government of the Founding Fathers, was the second paradigm that shaped our youthful existence in history. The Constitution of the United States is the paramount law of the nation and was designed to constrain future generations to live within its limits. For that reason, the Constitution provides long and difficult procedures for amending the Constitution, and includes checks and balances designed to protect against the usurpation of power. Having just fought a war against a powerful European monarch, our predecessors were distrustful of the Executive power. But, their experience during eight years under the Articles of Confederation taught them that state legislatures were also prone to usurpations of power—the enactment of unjust laws. As such, they were distrustful of the Legislative branch of the new national government and engaged in long discussions about how legislative abuses might be checked.

The Judicial power, Article III of the Constitution, and the literal words that make up the Constitution of the United States embedded the DNA of judicial review—the judicial act of interpreting the Constitution—as a basic aspect of all future American controversies. For that reason, some of the most difficult conflicts that divided the nation have been decided, not by the resolution of contending interests through war or legislation, but by changing the meaning of the Constitution itself. In some ways, this changing of the meaning of the Constitution's words can affect the existential meaning of our common existence. When those changes are contrary to the original intention of the Founding document, the central role given to the U.S. Supreme Court by the Constitution of the United States constitutes a continuing problem for contemporary American politics.

President Abraham Lincoln's "unsurpassable fusion of democratic symbolism with theoretical content," to use Eric Voegelin's description of the Gettysburg Address,[7] constituted a third paradigm, erupting during our early adulthood, enunciated at Gettysburg and in Lincoln's Second Inaugural. The United States had fought a destructive civil war that changed the character of the American people in ways that only the devastation of war can do. There is some evidence that the killing fields of Manassas, Fredericksburg, Chancellorsville, the Wilderness, Chickamauga and Gettysburg challenged the Christian beliefs of combatants on both sides. And Charles Darwin's *On the Origin of the Species* added religious doubt to the American soul. America had come out of the Civil War a secular nation, and Lincoln was its representative. America's third governing paradigm was, in some ways, conservative, but it carried the seeds of future disorder. Lincoln sought to preserve the Union, not destroy it, and challenged the Confederate notion of community based on a Lockean "compact" of states designed to protect private property and, of course, slaves. Lincoln fought a civil war to assure that "We the people of the United States" took precedence over any claims that a social contract between the American States formed the Union. But the revolutionary impulse of Jefferson's Enlightenment reasoning, mixed with Lincoln's new nationalism, emboldened by concentrated federal powers and fueled by civil war, sowed the seeds of a revolutionary fourth paradigm.

Abraham Lincoln was the forerunner of a truly revolutionary fourth paradigm of the American regime who, motivated by abhorrence of slavery, would fashion a civil religion that touched a responsive chord in his listeners because Lincoln's language was evocative of the King James Version. As Robert Kagan has noted, Lincoln borrowed from the religious "perfectionism" of the Second Great Awakening—"As your Father in Heaven is perfect, be ye also perfect."[8] We understand also from scholars who have

7   Ibid., p. 40.
8   Robert Kagan, *Dangerous Nation* (New York; Alfred A. Knopf, 2006). All citations from the Vintage Books paperback edition of *Dangerous Nation* (New York; Random House, 2007), p. 261.

studied modern millennialism that Lincoln spoke to a nation that had been prepared to understand its role as a "redeeming nation" by secular developments in the Protestant churches of the nineteenth century.[9] Lincoln's role was transitional, however.

President Woodrow Wilson's Progressive idealism fathered a political religion that became a fourth, thoroughly radical, paradigm that actualized the revolutionary potential of Lincoln's language and a secular democratic vision developed by Unitarian preachers responding to European nationalist movements and reflecting the deification of man of German idealism. If we might fight a civil war to make men free, might we not take the fight elsewhere to make men democratic? Thus it was that the only revolutionary paradigm to govern America was crafted by Woodrow Wilson and ultimately evolved into a regnant idealism that has fundamentally challenged the principles of limited government of the American regime from 1914 to the present day.

Under President Woodrow Wilson and his "Idealist" and "Progressive" successors, the American regime was transformed into a government of no limits, a limitless regime pursuing possible realities—much celebrated in the revival of the myth of Camelot by the Kennedy family—as opposed to a government grounded in real possibilities. Wilsonian idealism introduced an era of permanent revolution in which America sought to revolutionize world politics. Following Wilson's leadership, Progressives engaged in a permanent revolution aimed at overcoming American traditions, traditional society and the remnants of Christianity. Through them, an aggressive idealism was fashioned that sought not truth, but power to engage in revolutionary acts that would replace reality with another, "second reality,"[10] more to their pleasing.

9   Ernest Lee Tuveson, *Redeemer Nation: The Idea of America's Millennial Role* (University of Chicago Press, 1968), 205–6. Richard Gamble, "Gettysburg Gospel," The American Conservative, November 14, 2013 and "The Battle Hymn of the Republic and American Civil Religion," *Modern Age* (Fall, 2014).
10   Ellis Sandoz, *The Collected Works of Eric Voegelin*, Vol. 145 (Baton Rouge:

The Conservative Rebellion as we know it, therefore, is not a dumb reaction to more than a century of Wilsonian "Idealism" culminating in the presidency of Barack Obama. It is the equivalent of an organism's recovery from disease; a living community striving to recover the truth of the American political experience and our history; a paradigm of such vitality that it may constitute a fifth governing paradigm in the history of the American democratic republic.

For that reason, the Conservative Rebellion—its ideas and constructs, experience and history—as it is treated here—is not some isolated aspect of the American nation's political history, nor a mere idea, but the intellectual form through which the American nation itself is striving to renew itself by shedding a previous self-interpretation.

The weekend that the Berlin Wall fell in November, 1989, I was in Warsaw, Poland and I reflected at that moment on the basic truth that the Berlin Wall didn't fall by one fitful burst of outrage at the absurdities of Communism and the centralized bureaucratic state that was East Germany. It fell from the weight of the suffering and the shattered aspirations of millions of human beings over forty years of Soviet hegemony. We Americans were spared a similar fate, and as I worked my way through Warsaw airport's passenger terminal to my return flight to Munich, I thanked God for the privilege of having had the opportunity to live in America and to have had the opportunity to stand, alongside my conservative brethren, in opposition to the Soviet Union and the Progressives who have dominated American politics in my lifetime.

In this study, I travel two paths. The first recalls a twenty-year period—from the presidency of John F. Kennedy to the presidency of Jimmy Carter—in which my fellow Conservative Rebels and I participated in the Rebellion. During that time, the outcome

Louisiana State University Press, 1990), *Autobiographical Reflections*, p. 212. Voegelin translated the term "another reality" in Robert Musil's *A Man Without Qualities* into English as "second reality."

of the presidential election of 1980 could not have been predicted. But, irrespective of the outcome of these practical events, we found our voice, came to a common understanding of our history and the world, and looked for the leadership that represented our values.

We Conservatives Rebels had little expectation during the time of our rebellion that a conservative leader would become President of the United States, nor did we anticipate that the Soviet Union would collapse and that, after that collapse, questions would be asked about our cohesiveness as a political movement. Even as late as November, 1980, conservatives could meet in convention in Washington, Chicago, New York, or New Orleans, share the common bonds of friendship and a common anti-Communism, and wish one another well. That changed in 1980 and, again, in 1991.

Friendships were strained by the in-fighting for prominence that is an inevitable by-product of political ascendancy that occurred with the election of Ronald Reagan. But, also, after the demise of the Soviet Union, there occurred a rise of sectarian enthusiasms that threatened to impose a confessional standard on American politics. And when joined with the lust to make the world safe for democracy, some became advocates for imperial wars. In that condominium of millenarian Christians and Neoconservatives, the fourth paradigm rose again to challenge the fifth.

The second path I travel is one for which I was trained by my experience and graduate education under the tutelage of Stanley Parry, CSC,[11] Gerhart Niemeyer, Ralph McInerny and Eric Voegelin at the University of Notre Dame, and Michael Oakeshott at the London School of Economics.

At Notre Dame I discovered classical philosophy as an intellectual mode of "existence in truth."[12] There I learned that

---

11   Catholic religious orders identify their institutions by using acronyms: S.J.–Society of Jesus; C.S.C.–Congregation of Holy Cross.

12   Eric Voegelin, "On Debate and Existence," in *Published Essays 1966–1985*, *The Collected Works of Eric Voegelin*, Vol. 12 (Baton Rouge: Louisiana State University Press, 1990), p. 36.

philosophy is not a body of ideas, but, as Voegelin wrote, "a man's responsive pursuit of his questioning unrest to the divine source that has aroused it."[13] Thus I apply my knowledge as a political theorist to the central conflict facing America today: the battle for the American soul between fourth paradigm Wilsonian idealism and the fifth paradigm's Conservative Rebellion.

These reflections, therefore, introduce political philosophy to explain how ideas become actualized in civil society, the role of *daimonic* men and women in shaping and continuing our consciousness of order, and the possible loss of our consciousness of the sweep of Western thought through the decline of conservative scholarship and influence in academe. To that extent, my reflections are not one intellectual's story, but a philosophical reflection on a century of American experience as seen through the perspective of a participating intellectual in the Conservative Rebellion.

The eruption of conservative political ideas constitutes a living and vital attempt at recovery of political and social order that nourishes our great nation and should give us much hope for the future of America. The presence of men and women in civil society who are responsive to the *"daimon"*[14] in their souls, a term derived from Socrates' *daimon*, gives us hope that the American nation will attract the leadership needed to guide our country in the contest between the fourth and fifth paradigms that roil our culture, politics and religions. But, we must be attentive to troubles that lie just beneath the surface of the speeches of our political leaders, and look for a truer reality, the actions by which they actually live.

The dangers are twofold: If we turn our back on our common experience (or never experience the exhilaration of shared ideas) and give leadership to a new generation of neo-Wilsonians, we will enjoy only failure and great tragedy. And if we reject the

---

13 Eric Voegelin, *Works*, Vol. 12, "Reason. The Classic Experience," p. 272.

14 See my examination of this concept in "Daimonic Men," *Modern Age* (Winter, 1996), pp. 162–66. All citations from *Modern Age* are archived at **www.isi.org at the "Publications" tab**.

Christian faith that defines civilization in the West and seek a millennium in this world, we may find ourselves in a situation far worse than at any time in our history. There is a difference between "religion" and "faith," which I discuss in Chapter 6, and we need to keep that difference in mind. Of course, we are not solely political, economic, nor faithful, conservatives. We are Americans living a common history, within a common land, community, culture and traditions. Of the Conservative Rebellion which we share, this study has this to say: we Conservative Rebels are an important, new, phenomenon that is representative of the American community at this moment in its history—equivalent in many ways to the Americans who risked life and treasure to rebel against King George III in 1776. We are a community shaped in adverse circumstances by journalists such as Westbrook Pegler, George Sokolsky, and Felix Morley and given political influence by Robert Taft, who can be congratulated for evoking a national Conservative Rebellion. We are a community of conservatives whose commonality was articulated by post-World War II journals such as National Review, Human Events, and The Freeman, and by stubborn leaders such as Barry Goldwater. And we are a community of conservatives who became politically successful—for the first time in American history—only through the persistence of one ambitious and stubborn man, Ronald Reagan. If we are to learn from that experience, we must acknowledge that we are pygmies standing on the shoulders of these giants.

This is the "meat and potatoes" of what you are about to read. But, like most outlines, it doesn't reveal the intellectual struggle and growth of character needed to resist modern ideology that motivated me to work through an analysis of this problem of disorder and recovery of order in American civil society.

Eric Voegelin's recovery of our ability to think philosophically is, surely, central.

I can remember the exact day that I read, for the first time, a work by Eric Voegelin, *The New Science of Politics*, and my delight that thirty days later I would sit in his classes at the University of Notre Dame. But, also, even before that late November day in

1964—a bleak year for Conservative Rebels—I had the opportunity to meet and observe Bill Buckley, Russell Kirk, E. Victor Milione, Frank Meyer, Milton Friedman, Friedrich Hayek, William Rusher, Frank Chodorov, Leonard Read, Henry Regnery, and a host of other conservative intellectuals who may only be names to young people today. Had I been attracted, in advance of reading Eric Voegelin, to a rebellious rethinking of life? That is an important question because our Conservative Rebellion had a parallel in the '60s generation that sought revolutionary solutions.

What was it that caused an entire generation of post-World War II Americans to engage in revolution and their compatriots on the right to engage in rebellion?

Conservative Rebels, for certain, and Leftist revolutionaries of my generation quite possibly, smelled or sensed the moral collapse and the intellectual disorder of Progressive ideology that permeated American intellectual culture in the 1960s. How this generation interpreted that experience has shaped American life to this day.[15]

Clearly this is a theme that involves reflection on the disordered soul of Wilsonian idealism and a generation of Americans, sometimes called "the Greatest Generation," who sought to make a contribution to public life without a public philosophy. Confronted by the Great Depression. and enlisted into service in World War II, this generation came to appreciate the ability of collective action for the common good. Unfortunately, they mistook the symbolism of fourth-paradigm idealism for "good government," and harnessed generations that came later to government programs that hindered their freedom and mortgaged their income. Perhaps having encountered want and misery during the Great Depression and World War II, they were willing to give up

---

15 Nathan Glazer concluded that the student activists at Berkeley asserted insights "in forms that are new certainly for our times, and that speak with great force to people today in the moral, and yes, one may say it, in the spiritual sphere, their achievement is greater than in the political sphere." *Remembering the Answers. Essays on the American Student Revolt* (New York: Basic Books, 1970), p. 159.

some freedoms for security, but the generations that followed have had fewer chances to vote for the recovery of freedoms lost. When I look back at some of the failures of America's post-World War II leaders in politics, the arts, education and our churches, I have to ask myself, did this generation learn nothing?

In many ways, the best and the brightest of political leaders of that era showed in their daily remarks that they didn't have a clue about the nature of America as it faced that point in time when the fourth and fifth paradigms collided. We may try to analyze their pronouncements, but, in truth, in the final analysis we must conclude that Plato's theory of revolution of political forms is central to understanding our present predicament. The decline of the best regime that Plato explored by reference to changes in the character of those who constitute the regime seems to me more and more apt to the American situation. There is an American spirit, or "soul," and what influences affect the condition of that soul are critical to its recovery and renewal.

The state of university education in the 1960s—and now—assures that recovery of the order of the American soul will be elusive. That is what is troubling about the course of events in the United States since the civil disturbances of the late 1960s and early 1970s. The anti-Vietnam war movement was an opportunity not missed by ideologues who sought to transfer the elusive proletarian revolution to American colleges and universities. By taking control of colleges and universities students could be "educated" to become weapons used against the existing political order. This enlistment of American higher education in a cultural war against our common civilization has had devastating consequences. Today, as Dr. Russell Nieli demonstrates in a history of American higher education, the politicization of our higher education is complete.[16] Traditional core curricula have been

16 Russell Nieli, *From Christian Gentleman to Bewildered Seeker: The Transformation of Higher Education in America* (Raleigh: Pope Center for Higher Education Policy, 2007). **http://www.popecenter.org/acrobat/pope_articles/ fromchristiangentleman.pdf**

abandoned, replaced with ideologically-driven requirements or by cafeteria-style education that offers everything, but affirms nothing. That defines modern liberalism which affirms nothing, but offers everything.

As a "townie" riding to university classes by streetcar in Pittsburgh, I would notice advertisements on the sides of these cars that read, "College is America's Best Friend." I was certain that was a lie and "political correctness" on campuses today—a manifestation of totalitarianism in American form—reveals that the perpetrators of that lie are very much alive and well.

In reference to that experience of intellectual sickness, I see a need for a thorough critique of Wilsonian democratic idealism—the *ersatz* religion of our intellectual classes.

Though my recollections represent only one political theorist's perspective, these recollections transcend the merely personal and mediate an experience shared by millions of Americans who called themselves conservative during the last half of the twentieth century.

If I may anticipate a conclusion of my recollections, it is this: the future survival of the United States lies in learning from the generation of conservatives who joined the Conservative Rebellion in the 1950s, 1960s and 1970s and to those Americans living the Rebellion in the twenty-first century. This is an enormous topic that transcends what can be accomplished here and, so, I can only hope that I will have made a good beginning.

Chapter 2
Creation of a Conservative Rebel[1]

My first stirrings of Rebellion began with my experience of feeling intellectually ill at ease at that moment in American history that the administration of John F. Kennedy was inspiring thousands of young Americans to idealistic service on behalf of the state. We, my conservative colleagues and I, were representative of the future course that the American nation ultimately took, but, conversely, we were despised, denigrated, and rejected by our professors. That condescension by America's intellectuals remains a hallmark of America's colleges and universities.

These feelings of animosity were mutual, however, since we were dissatisfied with the view of America that dominated our professors' lectures. We didn't know why, but we knew that what they propounded was, quite simply, wrong. We were struggling, as was the nation, to understand ourselves, to make some sense of the intellectual poverty in which we found ourselves, and we were struggling to find our place in history and the world. In that sense, we thought we knew better than our professors, and we struggled to shape our own understanding of ethics, of American history and foreign policy, and to create values antithetical to those dominant in American intellectual circles. We lived in a divided country, dominated, on the one hand, by ideas of the "best and brightest" of our professors and transmitted to the larger American public through political elites, and the print and electronic media, and, on the other hand, an America whose outlines were only becoming clear in our mind's eye. We

---

1   This chapter is adapted from "The Creation of a Conservative Intellectual: 1960–65," Modern Age (Winter, 1998).

engaged in this reconstruction of America virtually at the same time that leftist students were engaged in the creation of new values and destructive New Left movements that would destroy the New Deal coalition that brought the Democratic Party to power and assure the election of Richard Nixon in the presidential election of 1968.

In reflecting on those times, my strongest recollection is that the ideas of America's intellectual elites did not resonate in my soul, and my later discovery that many of their most cherished beliefs were throwbacks to the Progressive era and could be traced to the political religion of Woodrow Wilson. Other ideas, ideas that sought not to understand, but to change, history, were imported from nineteenth-century European ideologies and mass movements. In other words, liberalism had nothing to say to the intellectual and spiritual needs of my generation, and we felt that our elected officials were mouthing platitudes that they no longer believed.

Structurally, America was fast becoming a centralized, bureaucratically administered state with power concentrated in Washington, and we were uncomfortable with that. There was also confusion about our goals as a nation, particularly in foreign affairs, and what our responsibilities were internationally. Our professors extolled the virtues of service to the state and the state's ability to secure the welfare of American citizens, but that appeal did not persuade us.

Before we knew that there was a "New Class," we were appalled by the Kennedy administration's failures in foreign policy, by the anti-business attitude of our professors, and we became concerned that no one took the Soviet threat seriously. The adulation showered upon President Kennedy by the American print media, moreover, was silly at best and ominous in its intensity. Kennedy's presidency was hardly the fulfillment of the American idea. And, as American Catholics were to learn later, John F. Kennedy was as secular a mind as ever graced the Oval Office. When the Administration-supported surrogate invasion of Cuba died at the Bay of Pigs due to an obvious failure of nerve on the part of the young president, I, like most Americans, recoiled in astonishment. This was followed by the president's loss of nerve in Berlin. We asked ourselves, "Why was this happening?"

Not that I had any answers myself.

Despite the creation of a union of Soviet satellite nations by brute military force, little was understood about Communist ideology. That political religion had a long philosophic history beginning in German idealism and the analysis of history of Karl Marx called dialectical materialism. Few Americans had studied that historical development and even fewer had studied Karl Marx, Frederick Engels or Vladimir Lenin. Thus denunciation of "Communism" was often contrasted to "Americanism." The sophisticated analyses of Albert Camus's *The Rebel* or Hannah Arendt's *Origins of Totalitarianism* published in 1951 had not penetrated our political classes or popular culture. I recall reacting negatively, for example, to the hoary anticommunist rhetoric of the American Legion that I encountered in my high school years as a debater and competitive orator at events sponsored by the American Legion. The defense of what was left of the American public philosophy had fallen to those who were intellectually unequipped. These good, honest, working-class men and women associated with these patriotic organizations were, simply, out of their league in a contest with the New York Times, Harvard professors, and a budding broadcast television media led by the likes of Edward R. Morrow, Chet Huntley, David Brinkley and Walter Cronkite. I was also repulsed by the rapid secularization of American society and the transfer of religious faith in salvation after death to salvation by social activism in this life. Prayer in the public schools was little substitute for religious training, yet even that had been ruled to be unconstitutional. America had chosen to run, not walk, towards a cultural crackup.

Popular culture in 1950s America was reflected in the popularity of Catholic Bishop Fulton Sheen whose weekly network television program launched in 1951 achieved an audience of Americans of all faiths. And FBI Director J. Edgar Hoover's 1958 classic warning about Soviet Communism, *Masters of Deceit,* reached an enormous audience because of Hoover's successful promotion of the Federal Bureau of Investigation. Hoover and Bishop Sheen were the only public figures who articulated a public philosophy to an American citizenry hungering for resolution of the intellectual confusion and conflicts of those times.

I now realize that I, too, was searching for some understanding of the historical moment and it was slowly dawning on me that the University of Pittsburgh—where, in September, 1960, I was enrolled as a freshman—was something very different from anything I had experienced before. I had known mundane corruption in my boyhood growing up in Pittsburgh. I saw money paid for votes and policemen take payoffs. Frankly, I was tolerant of all that, as I now see, because it didn't seem to affect the greater public good and because I understood that people always will act as the human beings they are.

But, the University of Pittsburgh was different. I sensed the presence of real spiritual disorder in the rejection of Christianity and the wisdom literature of the West, and the lack of reverence for the philosophy of limited government of the Founding Fathers. I also experienced, for the first time, an anger at the neglect of the important things in life by my professors. That anger, I believe, fueled the campus disturbances of the 1960s.

The University of Pittsburgh was—in microcosm—like all other universities in the United States, then and now, endowed with the same qualities that have occasioned over the years such books as Bill Buckley's *God and Man at Yale,* John LeBoutillier's *Harvard Hates America,* Roger Kimball's *Tenured Radicals* and Dinesh D'Souza's book on political correctness, *Illiberal Education.* I knew nothing of these matters when I applied to Pitt in 1960. Had I known better, I probably would have attended a small Lutheran college like Valparaiso in Indiana or the Presbyterian Grove City College. What I didn't know, I now realized, could and did hurt me—to the core of my being.

The University of Pittsburgh, long before I arrived, had developed into a secular institution whose social science faculty was dominated by the detritus of leftist intellectual and mass movements. Liberals, socialists, Marxists, behaviorists, members of the Communist Party, Comtean positivists, logical positivists, relativists, nihilists, all had converged at this particular institution. Pitt had become the largest employer in Allegheny County and had, literally, set itself up in opposition to the traditional culture that supported it.

The City of Pittsburgh at that time—with about 650,000 in population and half that today—evinced a tapestry of ethnic groups. Most Pitt students I met—like myself—were second-generation Americans. Polish, Irish, Italian, Ukrainian Catholic, Greek, Syrian and Russian Orthodox, German Lutheran, Jewish and Presbyterian houses of worship were everywhere and regular attendance at Mass, parish or Sabbath worship services was considered normal. Most of us were the first in our families to attend college. Yet the University's professoriate lived in another world. Daniel Patrick Moynihan's and Nathan Glazer's appreciative work on ethnicity had not been published, but if it had been, it would not have been at Pitt where deracinated social scientists abhorred the particular, the unique, as well as the diversity of Pittsburgh's religious and ethnic groups. They were committed to a larger, politicized agenda than that given in this city of traditional cultural, religious and social life and, of course, sports. Across from Pitt's cathedral of learning was Forbes Field, the home of the Pittsburgh Pirates. And up a very steep hill was Pitt Stadium that, at the time, was the home of the Pittsburgh Steelers and the University of Pittsburgh's Panthers. With the exception of Richard Mellon Scaife who had graduated from Pitt, few saw what was happening and he provided funding for world-class scholars to visit and teach traditional subjects. Wealthy immigrants who had made Pittsburgh their home were asked to contribute to exceptionally beautiful "nationality rooms" lavishly decorated to represent the ethnic groups that had immigrated to the region.

In Music Appreciation class, I remember that we examined any and all aspects of music, but my teacher appeared uncomfortable when students in class recognized that one of

Beethoven's themes was taken from a German hymn. Religion, according to this instructor, was for the "backward." For those sensitive students interested in contemplating the depth of the soul and who thirsted for knowledge about the human psyche, the Psychology Department at Pitt offered a Skinner Box. In fact, I earned five academic credits in a behavioral psychology course by conditioning a rat in a box named after Harvard psychologist B. F. Skinner. Over fourteen weeks I trained the rat by rewarding or denying it food. My Psychology professor believed the psychology of man, like rats, is defined by material causes.

In Political Science, my chosen major, I could choose courses from a wonderful array of liberals of all types and varieties, but not one political conservative. There was Democratic Party politician Ed Cook, who taught American state and local politics; New Deal Liberal, and Chairman of the Department Holbert N. Carroll, who taught Constitutional Law; positivist political theorist John Chapman; Carl Beck, master of "systems" theory—what I came to call the science of comparative rectangles—and an assortment of other left-of-center professors. Many years later, when I was teaching at the University of Dallas, I met Carl Beck at an annual convention of the American Political Science Association and decided that I might as well say hello. I introduced myself saying my name and extending my hand. Beck replied sneeringly, "I know who you are!"

Obviously, I had committed some offense when I was at Pitt, an offense that knew no name, back then.

I was "politically incorrect."

This atmosphere did not merely discriminate against young conservative undergraduates. I recall going to the office of distinguished linguist and visiting Mellon Professor at Pitt, Mario Pei, who was a regular contributor to *Modern Age,* to ask that he become faculty sponsor of the Society for Conservative Studies. Pei's annual essay in *Modern Age* on what he called "weasel words" made delightful fun of the ideological degeneration of our common language, but, confronted with a clear offer to assist some conservative students at the University of Pittsburgh, he told me that he would have to *think* about it. I returned in a week and Pei said that for him to sponsor our little conservative group would cause "trouble," and apologized that he couldn't lend his name to our efforts. Apparently, if the program of Visiting Professors funded by Dick Scaife was seen to be playing a role in fostering the Conservative Rebellion at Pitt, it would be difficult to sustain the program. There was outrage when Pitt granted authorization for a Youth for Goldwater rally on the lawn of the Cathedral of Learning.

I also recall that in my senior year I wrote an essay on Burke and John Randolph of Roanoke that was accepted for publication in the university's literary magazine, *Ideas and Figures.* Upon its publication, I discovered that editor Jeff Rackham, at the instigation of the very politically correct, had placed a footnote at the end of my essay that read:

> Editor's Note: The university is a place for the formation and free expression of ideas. The philosophy expressed in this article is not necessarily that of *Ideas and Figures,* but is published here in the belief that it will contribute to the further understanding of one area of political thought.

The title of my essay? *"A Vocabulary of Conservatism."* So blatantly politicized to the left was the environment at Pitt in 1964 that I couldn't publish a student's attempt at a scholarly essay on Edmund Burke and John Randolph of Roanoke without a politically correct disclaimer! I recall that I was blamed by a liberal classmate on the day President Kennedy died for creating the environment that led to the assassination of the President of the United States! No wonder my editors at *Ideas and Figures* felt that they were doing me a favor by allowing my essay to be published, but wanted to warn their readers that Bishirjian was possibly dangerous to free inquiry. An environment of supreme intolerance, to all but the politically correct, had been created at Pitt—an environment that continues today in most "academic" institutions in the

United States—and those of us who raised our heads in dissent became outcasts. Had I been informed in my political science classes about the theory of toleration, I would have asked myself, what had become of the liberal principle of toleration at the University of Pittsburgh? Only one more remembrance is needed to describe this madhouse of so-called "university" education that existed at Pitt.

The most notorious member of the History Department had fought in the Abraham Lincoln Brigade during the Spanish Civil War and Pitt had early attracted a Communist Party cell. A full accounting of this era can be obtained by calling the editorial offices of *The Washington Times* where a campus radical of the day, Ralph Hallow, now presides as a conservative journalist.

I erred when I decided to go to Pitt, and then I erred after I got there. It happened that the Chairman of the Physical Education Department was a member of my church and I was invited to meet him upon my arrival at Pitt. At the young age of eighteen and disgusted with the tedium and mindlessness of my high school education, the last thing I wanted to do was meet the Chairman of the Department of Physical Education at Pitt—and I told him as much.

Four years later, when I realized that only the English and the Physical Education Departments were committed to keeping body and soul together, I went to this same gentleman and apologized. I told him that I was wrong and that of all the departments at Pitt, I considered Physical Education to be the best. And I meant it.

It took me two years at Pitt to figure out which teachers to take and not to take. In the good column were English Department professors Richard Tobias, Charles Crow and Ralph Allen in Pitt's Theater Department. Allen would later produce the Broadway production of "Sugar Babies," and at Pitt directed Robert Penn Warren's "All the King's Men" in which I played the role of Willie Stark. With Tobias I took his course on Comedy and a directed reading course on Edmund Burke. With Crow I took his courses on poetry and Shakespeare. Those were the days before deconstructionism reigned supreme, and I recall telling Frank Meyer, a *National Review* editor we invited to speak at Pitt, that even though I was a political science major, I had more credits in English. "At least they couldn't ruin Shakespeare," I said, and Frank nodded in agreement. Also in the good column was an otherwise unappetizing professor, John Chapman, a positivist. Chapman had a precision of mind that attracted me to theoretical studies even though Chapman's political theory represented the last gasp of positivism. And though my grades were less than gentlemanly—it's tough learning falsehoods—Chapman's political theory courses helped me in my private reading.

From 1961 to 1964 I read any and every book I could get my hands on to try to figure out what in hell was going on. I sensed that some moral disease had afflicted our best educated classes, a corruption of the soul that had been transmitted to our political and cultural leaders also. But, I didn't yet understand why. My readings included almost every speech of Edmund Burke and his *Reflections on the Revolution in France*, Russell Kirk's *The Conservative Mind*, Peter Stanlis on Burke, Richard Weaver's *Ideas Have Consequences*, Friedrich Hayek's *Road to Serfdom* and his *Constitution of Liberty*, Frank Meyer, James Burnham, William F. Buckley, the essays of Stanley Parry and Mario Pei published in *Modern Age*, Ludwig von Mises' *Bureaucracy* and the history of economic thought. If it had been written and cited in *National Review, Modern Age* or the *Intercollegiate Review,* I read it. That's what curious undergraduates had to do, if they did not have conservative faculty to guide them.

Unfortunately, what I learned from my reading didn't quite hang together. Something was wrong and I attended ISI summer schools and lectures conducted by the Society for Conservative Studies to try and find out what was missing. As a result, I had the opportunity to meet personally Friedrich Hayek, William Rusher, Eliseo Vivas, Russell Kirk, Frank Meyer, Bill Buckley and Erik Maria Ritter von Kuehnelt-Leddihn from *National Review*. Liberalism, I now saw, was my adversary. Liberal ideology, as I later came to understand it, was a false idea that creative intellects had devised to replace reality, given in being, that they found unacceptable. Liberal ideology, unfortunately, is the dominant intellectual convention of the United States in my time and represents a significant current of deculuration of Western culture.

As such, Liberalism must be distinguished from the virtues of liberality, toleration, and magnanimity. Liberalism as I experienced it at Pitt was intolerant, illiberal, devoid of magnanimity and devoted to expansion of state power. "Why," Ed Cook, the Democratic Party politician who had a tenured position in Pitt's Political Science department, asked me in class, "don't you care for people?" "Professor, I responded, "I respect people and believe that if you leave them alone they'll do just fine. It is you who don't care for people because you want to control them."

Not bad for a twenty-year-old! On the other hand, I did not get an "A" in Ed Cook's course in state and local politics, nor did I care.

All my readings outside of my university courses were interesting, and had given me some good arguments, but I was no more than a debater looking for arguments to win points in public debates. Conservatism is not, by itself, a philosophy to live by, a way of truth. Important though it is for politics and economics—after all, it taught me about limited government and free markets and gave me an appreciation of constitutional restraints on power and the relationship between economic and political freedom—conservatism is a political theory linked to an attitude of spirit and mind, not a political *philosophy* by which the greater universe becomes visible and which, to me, was still invisible despite an enormous amount of reading.

My Lutheran religion didn't have the toughness of reason, the strength of argument and the rigor of human thought in quest of truth. I had lived twenty years and was about to graduate from university, but knew nothing of philosophy—not a word! As a result, I had not discovered that there is a philosophic mode by which the human intellect may participate in the divine. To be sure, I did experience God's presence through my prayer life and attendance as a communicant in my parish church. Unlike today where the Social Gospel is more likely to be taught at Mass, in chapel or synagogue, I, mercifully, could look to Sunday service as respite from the combative ideologies that were dominant in my university courses.

Yet my ignorance of philosophy was a tragic handicap and, in retrospect, it is clear that I had joined the "conservative movement" in an attempt to fill a perceived vacuum in my intellectual life. Let me offer a word of warning, however. "Movements" in the correct meaning of the word are not conservative and the conservative "movement" isn't really one.

Historically, "movements" are anti-traditional and ideologically motivated revolutionary currents. A typical "movement," for example, is Communism or National Socialism and they have distinct characteristics: 1) they reject reality; 2) they attribute the deficiencies in reality to others and make enemies of those "responsible"; 3) they promise resolution of the conflicts in existence; and 4) promise that when those conflicts are overcome history will have been concluded. "Communism is the riddle of history solved," is typical language by a "movement" leader such as Karl Marx.

Political conservatism in the United States doesn't fit the mold since it finds existence to be good and knows that no human action can fully conclude a process that transcends the limits of human history. Still, something was happening in American politics in 1961 and I had walked smack into it. By recognizing myself as a "movement conservative" I was simply giving a name, albeit an imperfect one, to something that I was living. Being a part of what we called the "conservative movement" was to recognize the social aspect of the political ideas that caused us to come together. We were a community and in that sense we should call this the "conservative community," not the conservative" movement."

So, even today, and being very uncomfortable in its usage, when we "movement" conservatives get together we often discuss how someone who is in a conservative government—say in the Reagan or Bush administrations—was not a "movement conservative." A host of luminaries in the Reagan and the first Bush administrations made it to the top, but without the philosophical commitment that such positions call for.

John Sununu, for example, who became George H. W. Bush's first chief of staff in 1989 is—intuitively—conservative, but he isn't a "movement" conservative.

In 1982 I was working as a legislative assistant to Senator Alfonse M. D'Amato (R-NY), when D'Amato's pollster and my friend of many years, Arthur Finkelstein, called and asked me to arrange a lunch with a young politician/educator from New Hampshire, John Sununu. I took Sununu to lunch at the Hunan Restaurant across from the Hart Senate Office Building. We ordered Kung Pao chicken, fried dumplings, and Hunan beef and I listened as Sununu told me about his children, his academic and consulting career, and his political aspirations. "Dick," Sununu told me, "I am going to run for Governor of New Hampshire so I can block Jim Baker from getting the Republican presidential nomination for George Bush." What explains why Sununu accepted employment with a President who, seven years earlier, he rejected because he was not a political conservative?

Throughout the presidency of Ronald Reagan, my friends and I could discern the differences between those who were allegedly conservative and those few "movement" conservatives who had been given the opportunity to serve President Reagan. We were acknowledging a kinship with one another, a sharing in a common enterprise of which we were very proud and yet, in the technical sense, we knew that that of which we were a part was different from a political "movement" or "cause." The term "cause" was first critically used by Richard Hooker in his opus, *Ecclesiastical Polity*, to describe the destructive effects of the Puritan "cause." No, we conservatives weren't engaged in destructive actions of that sort and we sensed that we were a part of the regenerative life of the nation itself.

Something, clearly regenerative, had been astir in the United States since Robert Taft—too late to equip the nation intellectually to engage the murderous Stalin and Mao Tse-tung with policies more vigorous than the policies America's liberal elites pursued—but this regenerative, restorative force hadn't yet come into its own. That historical development, which was still in process in 1961, is the regenerative force that we have now come to call the Conservative Rebellion.

In its inarticulate form, however, conservatism can be easily portrayed as mindless, "reactionary"—whatever that pejorative means—and negative. In, truth, there exists a body of knowledge that makes up a consistent political philosophy in America that deserves the name "conservative." Unfortunately, a cultural process in the West, in development since the French Revolution, has attracted our finest intellects to destruction as opposed to recovery.

Why are most creative people, artists, writers, journalists and academics not philosophical conservatives? This question is often asked, and the answer is simply that, since the seventeenth century, at least, the creative among us have been encouraged by cultural currents to reject traditional society and institutions and to replace them with institutions that are "better," "more open," "new," "revolutionary," and which promise to reconcile and transcend the conflicts of existence. In twentieth-century America, only since Robert Taft did we conservatives begin to shape a political philosophy and become an effective social force to defend traditional American institutions, traditions, and attitudes from these attacks. In doing so, those who participate in this creative act are replicating a similar restorative force that gave shape to the War of Independence and the Founding of the American Constitution. The "Spirit of '76" that inspired a heroic rebellion is uniquely American and equivalent to the rebellion against liberalism that took place in the United States after World War II.

Nevertheless, rebellions, like revival meetings, need institutional structure. The War of Independence did not automatically convey a working political system to replace colonial rule. That was the task of the Founders who engaged in the political debates leading up to the Philadelphia Convention and the ratification debates. Modern political conservatives take inspiration from both the War of Independence and the American Founding. And I have come to believe that the Conservative Rebellion which led me and thousands of others to rebel against the dominant ideology of America in the twentieth century has much in common with the Spirit of '76. But, of course, modern conservatism and the eighteenth-century War of Independence are not the same thing.

The twentieth-century Conservative Rebellion is of a kind by itself, wholly new, philosophically deeper, and responsive to the current crisis, not the past. In responding to that crisis a great deal of time, thought and energy has been given to critiquing the absence of a coherent political philosophy, the reigning liberal ideology and the many ills with which that ideology has infected the American people, including ethical relativism and economic policies for redistributing wealth. The generation that founded our country could and did rely on an Enlightenment consensus that gave them the political ideas used to justify their rebellion. They did not need to create a consensus, but merely apply the existing one in new ways. We, however, were not so blessed, or, put another way, we realized that the Enlightenment contained the seeds of deculturation of the Western Christianitas and had to be replaced.

But, with what?

Commencing in the 1950s and 1960s, conservatives in the United States gave a great deal of emphasis, labor, thought and time to recovery of a philosophical tradition that went far beyond the Enlightenment. We conservative students of that period participated in that restorative effort by acquiring the intellectual and philosophic skills to oppose the idea of our professors. That was what we were challenged to do, and which we accomplished. But, it wasn't easy.

What I am suggesting is that something was afoot at that moment in American history, 1960–65, that led tens of thousands of working-class students to find their voices and fashion themselves into an intellectual and political force. We were not made into conservatives out of whole cloth, however. We came to university with fundamental values, faith and beliefs that were challenged by intolerant liberal professors who disdained our religion, our love of country, our acceptance of authority, and, in facing up to that challenge, we found our voice.

Let me ask here, what was it that we had in common, that bound us together and that shaped our response to the challenges presented by our teachers? For myself, and the majority of the conservative students I met during my intellectual journey, that common tie was not only modest means, but acceptance of authority, an appreciation of hard work, and the reality of Christian faith. Not all our Christian colleagues or students from working-class families became conservatives, but very few were atheists.

On the Left, also, amongst the secular souls who would become known as the "Sixties Generation," a spiritual migration was occurring. A profusion of organizations competed for the attention of colleges students: Students for a Democratic Society (SDS), an outgrowth of a socialist student organization that sought to use university students as weapons in a war against capitalism; the Student Nonviolent Coordinating Committee (SNCC) that engaged in civil rights activism; the anti-Vietnam War movement that developed from the University of California-Berkeley "Free Speech Movement" and the Woodstock Festival, and collectively prepared them for social and political action even as we conservatives rallied for Barry Goldwater.

But, by what forces?

Certainly, the failure to fashion an effective public philosophy by the generation of the Great Depression and World War II left a vacuum in American public and intellectual life that we of the Right and the Left were, unbeknownst to us, attempting to fill with new ideas and new forms. The key in the radicalization of our fellow liberal students was their college and university professors who had turned them against their fathers' intellectual neglect. We conservative students, however, were fighting in defense of the American experience against those who sought to trash it. The liberal students of the day were converted by their professors from conservative values to the values of relativism, collectivism, statism, and the belief that state power should be captured for the advancement of an ideology. We, without faculty mentors we could trust, chose to defend God, country, and home.

This total rejection of traditional culture by our peers and university professors had its mirror image in our enthusiasm for Sen. Barry Goldwater. Intuitively, we understood that it was necessary to support Barry Goldwater and that though he was reluctant, at first, to seek the mantle of leadership of the Republican Party, these were times that required courage, and we sensed that Goldwater would, ultimately, run. I remember those days vividly because it was clear that President Lyndon Johnson was not telling the truth about his commitment, nor the magnitude of the commitment needed, to win the war in Vietnam. Not only that, we were not told why we had men fighting in Vietnam, except for some mention, as I recall, of the "right to self-determination." In reality, Johnson had not thought the matter through, was not committed to fight to win, and wasted the lives of 58,300 Americans killed in action in Vietnam, all in the name of an ideology that failed in 1918!

"Self-determination" is a Wilsonian ersatz principle of international relations that stands opposed to the true principle of statecraft—"national interest." Our national interest should govern our actions in foreign affairs. Only after a careful and full consideration of the American national interest, I should say only after prudential consideration, and when the national interest can be articulated so that the American people understand, only then should we put American troops in the line of fire. It is certainly good for nations to determine their own fate. But, it is not a moral obligation of the American people to die so that others may realize their nationhood.

For that reason, I was most uncomfortable during the first Bush administration when President Bush justified foreign intervention in response to the actions of "dictators." That too is a Wilsonian pejorative that interprets international relations in terms of a theology of democracy and justifies any and every American intervention abroad by an appeal to morality. Too often, those appeals to actions that are contrary to the national interest are couched in moralistic arguments.

That is not to say that we should not have been engaged in a war in Southeast Asia, say, on behalf of the national interest of the United States. But all the necessary thinking, analysis and presentation of that proposition to the American people had not been done. Nor had there been a commitment to pursue a strategy of winning the war. In fact, there was very little thought beforehand, no commitment to win, and much lying to the American people by such "moralists" as President Lyndon Johnson, U.S. Secretary of Defense Robert McNamara, and, yes, President John F. Kennedy. This is not my opinion. The American people recognized that as a fact, rejected the Democratic Party's leadership in foreign policy and denied Democrats the American presidency for a quarter of a century from, essentially, 1969 when Richard Nixon defeated Vice President Hubert Humphrey to the defeat of George Herbert Walker Bush by William Jefferson Clinton in 1992. I omit the defeat of President Gerald Ford by Jimmy Carter in 1976 because Watergate had tainted the Republican Party with the brush of scandal.

The 1964 presidential campaign was a truly "ideological" war, waged on American soil, in which the nation was told that the election contest between President Lyndon Johnson and Arizona Senator Barry Goldwater was a contest between the forces of light and the forces of darkness. And, like all ideologically imposed divisions, with it came a violation of the basic civility, toleration and statesmanship with which democratic contests ought to be waged. From that experience in 1964 came myriad changes in attitudes that mark politics in our time as the dirtiest business on earth—unsuitable for men of principle. The media's loss of objectivity and lock-step negative reporting of the Goldwater campaign effort ignored Lyndon Johnson's control of corporate campaign contributions through the threat of termination of defense contracts and the secret planning to expand the numbers of American troops in Vietnam—and *we*, the conservatives, were effectively portrayed as "Fascists"!

Clearly, the American establishment, including our university instructors who did not honor the title "Professor," the print and electronic media and the political establishment, including Pennsylvania's Republican Governor, Bill Scranton, and the liberal wing of the Republican Party led by Governor Nelson Rockefeller of New York, were not about to allow an avowed conservative become president of the United States. That precious promontory was reserved for folks like them—not us.

We who worked in that campaign were witnesses to the orchestration of all the forces of intellectual liberalism and liberal culture to repel the invasion from the heartland, and deny the American people the awareness that they had a straightforward choice between two distinct philosophies of government.

"A Choice, Not an Echo," Goldwater's campaign theme, was true only in the sense of what Goldwater intended. Goldwater wanted to offer the American people a choice between limited government, free enterprise and the strict construction of the Constitution versus the politics of an intrusive, bureaucratic, centrally administered state led by a man who had enriched himself and his family by abuse of his political office.

Against the juggernaut led by President Johnson stood Barry Goldwater, who knew he would lose, but chose to run rather than give up the contest to a man he called a "crook." But, instead of having the opportunity to offer the American people a choice for limited government, Goldwater was portrayed as a malicious simpleton with vague longings for the military system of Hitler's Germany and an aching to plunge the world into nuclear war!

On Tuesday, November 3, 1964, the demonization of Goldwater was over. Lyndon Johnson had won the presidential election. That week, I picked up my copy of Eric Voegelin's *New Science of Politics* that I had ordered from Pitt's bookstore, went home, and waited for the acceptance letter from Notre Dame's graduate program in Government.

I had an abiding passion for politics and political theory, however, and I read with interest Fr. Stanley Parry's essays on tradition and American political thought that appeared in *Modern Age.*

Fr. Parry, C.S.C, was a member of the Congregation of Holy Cross, the University of Notre Dame's founding religious order, and Chairman of the Department of Government.

Now, here was a place, surely, that would give me a break from the beating I had taken at Pitt. I sent off my application, and wrote a letter to Stanley Parry in which I enclosed a long paper on Edmund Burke that I had written for Professor Richard Tobias, and waited while I turned to Voegelin's *New Science* of *Politics*.

Eric Voegelin published *The New Science* of *Politics* in 1952. Originally given as six lectures on "Truth and Representation" at the University of Chicago in Winter, 1952 under the sponsorship of the Charles R. Walgreen Foundation, Voegelin's editors at the University of Chicago Press gave the book its misleading title. Twelve years later, I came upon the book and I asked myself, why hadn't one of my professors at Pitt—when I was there from 1960 to 1964—recommended it to me? Why, indeed! As I read the book, I realized that at work was a substantial intellect far greater than any I had encountered in my readings or university classes. But, more particularly, even though I did not comprehend ninety percent of what I was reading, I did comprehend the essence of parts of it. In particular, Voegelin discusses the civilizational process in which the Christian expectation of spiritual fulfillment after death becomes immanentized in intellectual and political movements that seek a this-worldly salvation. Voegelin remarks that his analysis seems "rather elemental,"[2] and asks why, if this is the case, didn't the theorists who formulated these movements see the fallacy? Since he couldn't explain "seven centuries of intellectual history by stupidity and dishonesty," what was the reason? I then read the passage I have read many, many times and to which, invariably, literally thousands of commentators on Voegelin return:

> Ontologically, the substance of things hoped for is nowhere to be found but in faith itself; and, epistemologically, there is no proof for things unseen but again

2   Eric Voegelin, *The New Science of Politics*, p. 121.

this very faith. The bond is tenuous, indeed, and it may snap easily. The life of the soul in openness toward God, the waiting, the periods of aridity and dullness, guilt and despondency, contrition and repentance, for-sakenness and hope against hope, the silent stirrings of love and grace, trembling on the verge of a certainty which if gained is loss— the very lightness of this fabric may prove too heavy a burden for men who lust for massively possessive experience.[3]

Nothing I had read to that moment, or thereafter, moved me more than this two- sentence passage and I knew, suddenly, that I had found the intellectual guide I had sought for so long. And, I began to cry. Perhaps that describes how much we Conservative Rebels were seeking to overcome the dominant political religion of America in the 1960s. What I did not reckon upon was that in little more than a month and a half, arriving in South Bend, Indiana in January, 1965, I would be sitting in Voegelin's graduate seminar on modern political thought and auditing his undergraduate class.

South Bend, Indiana, is one of those unfortunate geographic locations where Catholic religious orders sometimes found insti-tutions. The Jesuits, to their credit, tend to locate their universities near centers of population—and power—such as Washington, D.C. (Georgetown) Boston (Boston College), and the Loyola Uni-versities of Chicago, New Orleans and Los Angeles, as well as New York (Fordham), San Francisco (University of San Fran-cisco). The Congregation of the Holy Cross, alternatively, sought remote, provincial sites, and South Bend, Indiana, fit the bill.

This geographic and intellectual backwater also had the dis-tinct disadvantage of extremes of hot and cold weather, including blinding snowstorms, hurricane force winds and tornadoes. A more unsatisfactory place for human habitation and the life of the mind—especially my habitat and my mind—could not have been found by otherwise intelligent souls.

3   Ibid., p. 122.

Upon my arrival at South Bend airport from Pittsburgh, which by comparison seemed like a major city, the temperature was seventy degrees. When I awakened the next morning, I had to buy a pair of galoshes since a foot of snow had fallen. That experience with South Bend was typical. On the other hand, I wasn't there to do anything but study. My tenure was probationary. Bad grades, even those earned from long suffering under intolerant professors, are, still, bad grades. Also, I barely had enough money to pay for tuition, books, rent for a room and meals in the cafeteria. Dining in town was out of the question. In one single instant, this otherwise intelligent young man had reduced the quality of his life by fifty percent—at least.

I was ecstatic!

I couldn't wait to enroll in the classes of Stanley Parry, Eric Voegelin, and Gerhart Niemeyer, a more compatible group of intellects than I had ever been honored to meet. Little did I know, however, that these were men under siege. Fr. Parry had been removed from his position of Chairman of the Department of Government by the calculated act of a committed liberal secular mind who happened to be President of the University, Fr. Theodore Hesburgh. Hesburgh had made a decision to "upgrade" the university and Stanley Parry, C.S.C, was in his gun sights.

Even good old Democratic Party politician, Ed Cook, my American politics professor at the University of Pittsburgh, knew who Fr. Parry was when I told him that I was going to Notre Dame. Fr. Parry had lent his name to a number of conservative political organizations, including the late presidential campaign of Barry Goldwater, and it must have caused Reverend Hesburgh great discomfort when the head of the Rockefeller Foundation in New York told him that his university was a haven for right-wingers like Fr. Parry.

Parry had to go—and he did.

The presidents of universities run by religious institutions of the time didn't pay courtesy calls. The decisions they made stuck. Hesburgh had to rid his university of conservatives—after all, his former law dean, Clarence Manion, was continuing to embarrass Hesburgh by his popular radio program, "Manion Forum of the

Air," featuring none other than the former Dean of the University of Notre Dame's Law School. Dean Manion's radio program must have stung Hesburgh badly, as did other encounters with members of Notre Dame's faculty who were prominent conservatives. On one occasion, Hesburgh and other university presidents were invited to Washington to hear a briefing on foreign policy at the Department of State, and out walked Professor Gerhart Niemeyer.

Hesburgh didn't have to travel to Washington to see the likes of Niemeyer and he must have prayed nightly to be rid of these idiots who were costing him big bucks. The "smart" money wasn't going to universities that featured prominent conservatives. The association of Catholicism and Notre Dame in the popular mind with anti-communism was just too much for this secular-minded liberal, Democratic Party supporter, Kennedy family friend, favorite of the liberal elite, political appointee, jet-setter and, yes, fundraiser extraordinaire, Fr. Theodore Hesburgh, C.S.C. Thirty years ago, Fr. Hesburgh and all the other presidents of Catholic Universities in the world met in Rome with Pope John Paul II. They sat in a circle with the Pontiff who gave each an opportunity to introduce himself and summarize his expertise. When it came to Fr. Hesburgh's turn, he identified himself and announced that his expertise was raising money!

For a good Catholic fundraiser in President John F. Kennedy's America, apparently, football was okay; but not anti-communism, nor even philosophical conservatism.

My first experiences with the "new" Notre Dame were enlightening.

The newly appointed Chairman of the Department of Government was a specialist in Latin American studies, John Kennedy. A big, affable, liberal Democrat with a sensitive and intelligent face, Kennedy was Hesburgh's choice to succeed Fr. Parry as Chairman of the Department. At that historical moment, Fr. Parry, Voegelin and Niemeyer constituted the strongest faculty in political theory in America, and, with the exception of Voegelin's group at the University of Munich, most probably in the world. With four more careful additions—most certainly not

Kennedy—Notre Dame could have become the strongest political theory department in the nation. That title would soon go by default to the University of Chicago where Leo Strauss presided, and later to Claremont Graduate School, where Leo Strauss's students, principally Harry Jaffa, Martin Diamond and others, congregated. Instead, Fr. Hesburgh allowed liberal political ideology to dominate his judgment and turned over the Department of Government to conventional minds. That was bad enough, but Hesburgh's hand-picked Chairman, Kennedy, decided to use his resources to build a Latin American studies program. Latin America?

Take a backwater graduate institution along the St. Joseph River like Notre Dame, have it focus on a backwater region like Latin America, and you seal Notre Dame's fate as just another graduate program in Government. For that, we may thank the Rev. Theodore Hesburgh.

Since I was arriving at Notre Dame in mid-term—American presidential elections, unlike Congress, do not follow the academic year—I had to gain personal permission to enter Niemeyer's graduate course, appropriately titled "Communist Ideology," in mid-term.

Niemeyer was a German émigré who fled Nazi Germany, first to Spain and then to the United States. He had been trained in jurisprudence in Germany, became a specialist in international law and served in the U.S. Department of State. His contract at Princeton was not renewed, however, when, in response to a colleague's playing the *Internationale* on the piano at a faculty party, Niemeyer responded by playing the *Star-Spangled Banner.* Niemeyer was a gifted theorist and a gifted musician. If only he had not been a musician, he might have been allowed by his intolerant colleagues to remain at Princeton.[4]

4   Niemeyer told me of the musical incident and its aftermath as reported here. A different version is given by Niemeyer's son, Paul Niemeyer, in *A Path Remembered. The Lives of Gerhart and Lucie Niemeyer* (Wilmington: ISI Books, 2006) p. 223.

So, when Notre Dame's Chairman, Fr. Parry, offered Niemeyer a position at Notre Dame in 1955, he accepted. Notre Dame, at the time, was an extraordinary institution that carefully took the best émigré talent with an affinity for Catholic education, including Waldemar Gurian, founder and editor of the *Review of Politics*; Theodore Kertesz, the former Hungarian diplomat, teaching international relations; Niemeyer in political theory; the theologian and political theorist J. H. Bochenski; Eric Voegelin, and many others.

My first meeting with Niemeyer was an experience to remember. Niemeyer was well known for his seriousness, his awareness of the "class" distinction between students and faculty, and the difficulty of his courses. I also sensed something more when I met him since, arriving as I did in mid-semester, he astutely asked me where I had been. I immediately thought that I better have the right answer. Telling him, for example, that I needed a break from undergraduate school wouldn't be good, nor was it true. He needed to know also that I had not been recently released from jail. So, even though I was gun-shy from the campaign in which working for Goldwater was a social stigma, I owned up and told him that I had just finished work on the Goldwater campaign and couldn't go to school in September. I really didn't know Niemeyer, and I wasn't quite sure that this was the best approach. But, it was the truth. Much to my surprise, his voice became less stern and he said, "Well, welcome aboard," and invited me to dinner at his home. "Dinner at Niemeyer's home? Are you joking?," my new classmates asked. "No student is ever invited to Niemeyer's home." I then knew that I was, indeed, "home."

Chapter 3
Home

The rebellion of modern American intellectual conservatism is spiritually akin to the rebellion symbolized in the "Spirit of '76." But, instead of the limitations of Enlightenment reasoning unsympathetic to Christianity that adversely affected some eighteenth-century American colonial leaders, many modern conservatives were fortunate to participate in, and become the beneficiaries of a recovery of classical Greek philosophy. That philosophy, which was open to the divine presence in reality, enabled us to reconcile our reason with our religious experience.

That was the "home" where I found myself in winter 1965, astonished that I was soon to attend a seminar on Modern Political Theory with Eric Voegelin, a seminar on Communist Ideology with Gerhart Niemeyer, and a seminar with Stanley Parry, C.S.C., on St. Augustine and Thomas Hobbes.

We mid-twentieth-century Conservative Rebels fortunate enough to enroll in Notre Dame's graduate program in Government understood that we were given the opportunity to recover the wisdom, foresight, and prudence of the Founding Fathers who shaped the Constitution of the United States and to integrate philosophical truth into our defense of tradition.

Beginning in the 1960s, we saw how Enlightenment symbols of rights, equality and liberty became autonomous from the rule of law and used as pretexts for New Left license and nihilism. It has taken my generation of conservatives fifty years to recover the intellectual ground that enables Conservative Rebels of today to articulate a way to recovery of political order.

We modern conservatives were forced to fashion new intellectual ground to support ordered liberty against the onslaught of modern ideologies at home and totalitarianism abroad. During the twentieth century, perhaps the bloodiest in the history of mankind, East, Central and Western Europe had been subjected to revolutions and a succession of wars that destroyed the Austro-Hungarian, Russian, German and Ottoman empires. The descent into a frenzy of madness and destruction in East and Central Europe led, little more than a quarter century later, to a second World War and saw the occupation of France and the survival of England seriously threatened. When monarchies were overthrown and replaced with totalitarian regimes, the United States was compelled to fight a succession of wars from World War II, the Korean War, to the war in Vietnam. Nothing grows more quickly during war than the powers of the state with the result that by the end of the twentieth century the American administrative state had become the enemy of all Americans, but only social, political and economic conservatives seemed concerned.

In the United States, the intellectual recovery that was required to analyze and seek to resolve the threat to American freedom of the administrative state took place at Notre Dame under the influence of Eric Voegelin, Gerhart Niemeyer, and Stanley Parry, and at the University of Chicago with Leo Strauss.

Two works that symbolize that recovery are Eric Voegelin's *New Science of Politics* and Leo Strauss's *Natural Right and History*. But, I get ahead of myself.

At Notre Dame, my new "home" under the tutelage of Eric Voegelin, Gerhart Niemeyer and Stanley Parry, and later Ralph McInerny, was an invitation to metamorphose into something entirely different from that which I had been, into something I did not even know existed.

As an undergraduate at the University of Pittsburgh, I had worked for the county Republican Party, pursued the role of a conservative activist on campus, worked on the Goldwater campaign for President, and plotted a future political career in Pennsylvania. Had I pursued that course, my career would undoubtedly have included law school and a successful run for the Pennsylvania state legislature, and, probably, a criminal indictment. Politics in my home town of Pittsburgh and in the Commonwealth of Pennsylvania was thoroughly corrupt. Sitting judges took retainers from their former law firms. Voter registration lists and voting machines were rigged. Members of the state legislature supplemented their income with bribes. By the grace of God, I was intellectually curious, even anxious, to find answers to fundamental questions about the intellectual confusion of the historical moment in which I lived, and, frankly, the ignorance of the American electorate who voted for what would soon become a disastrous and tragic end of the Kennedy presidency.

I was compelled to satisfy a thirst to comprehend what it was that created the historical predicament of the Cold War and the willingness by both political parties to grow the powers of an American government which, I believed, threatened to doom my country to despotism.

At the University of Pittsburgh, few shared my judgment that the United States had not responded to the challenge of the Soviet Union in Cuba and Berlin and that the United States was a nation in peril, and no one told me that a course of intellectual recovery existed. My behaviorist professors in Psychology, liberal professors in Political Science, and Marxist graduate assistants in the Department of History were representatives of a deformed consciousness, not the solution to a spiritual disease that infected our intellectual classes, who were ignorant of the fact that they were ignorant.

The intellectual challenge that I encountered at Notre Dame, therefore, opening the doors to classical philosophy as it did, challenged me to understand the originating experiences that led to the development of philosophy in ancient Greece. Recovery of classical philosophy was in process in the writings of my political theory teachers at Notre Dame: Eric Voegelin, Gerhart Niemeyer and Stanley Parry.

They had done my homework for me, had plowed the road, but left me alone to travel in the direction that road went. What they discovered could not be reduced to propositions, but required that I live a life of analysis, contemplation and reflection.

I had them as an example and could follow in their footsteps, but the task ahead would be far more consuming than I had any reason to comprehend when I first arrived in South Bend.

After making that journey of three hundred and eighty miles from Pittsburgh, Pennsylvania to South Bend, Indiana, I could not return to where I had been born and raised, and simply pick up life where I left lt. I was to set course on an intellectual journey deep into the recesses of the human soul and mind, of human history and artifacts of ancient civilizations, and there to recover experiences of reality that had been occluded by American secular culture. During the years that followed, I began to learn to interpret those experiences, analyze the present historical moment, and apply that experience to a political philosophy that would outline the limits of state power. This was political theory, not conservative political theory, but identifying freedoms threatened by our administrative state placed us in opposition to those who wanted that state apparatus to grow in beneficent powers, programs, and policies. Saying that this couldn't be done made us conservative.

That was the burden carried by the students of Eric Voegelin, Gerhart Niemeyer, and Stanley Parry who participated in the Conservative Rebellion.

That way, for me, was other than anything I had experienced in my youthful spiritual and religious life, and explains why religion, though important by itself, is not sufficient intellectually for us to heal and recover from the intellectual diseases of the soul that plague the modern West.

In following a philosophic path under Voegelin's, Niemeyer's and Fr. Parry's guidance, I discovered that my spiritual and intellectual life were not contrary to one another, but traveled along parallel courses to equivalent experience. And I would later apply these truths to American politics, constitutional history and the history of American political thought.

In an America fast becoming completely secularized and dominated by an expansive, spiritually diminished, bureaucratic administrative state, I was fortunate enough to encounter the one

American school of political philosophy in my lifetime that was open to the divine presence in reality.

At Notre Dame, at that moment in time, in the recesses of the Department of Government and surrounded by representatives of Thomistic propositional metaphysics in the throes of being remaindered by a Catholic Church rushing toward a cultural crackup, our teachers pursued truth without impairment by the acid of skepticism, ideology and dogmatism and were sowing the seeds of a political renaissance that I now call the Conservative Rebellion.

Of these three teachers who influenced me in the Department of Government at Notre Dame (Voegelin, Niemeyer and Parry), only Father Stanley Parry was a Roman Catholic. The irony of that ecumenical event never fails to amaze me. I was raised a Lutheran in a working-class family of first-generation American parents who had no ties to ethnic Irish or Italian Catholics, nor to "Catholic culture." With absolutely no previous contact with American Catholics, especially Catholic priests, I little knew what to expect. I completely missed out on the experience of my Notre Dame classmates who had attended twelve years of Catholic elementary and secondary schooling. Perhaps for that reason, I still find myself more at home among European Catholics than the American variant, and among priests or clergy of any faith I am, like most conservatives who take theology seriously, extremely uncomfortable. Frederick Wilhelmsen[1] once explained that to me in these words, "Conservatives are anti-clerical."

But, that is another story.

Suffice it to say, twenty years after the end of World War II, I found myself in the bowels of one of America's premier Catholic educational institutions where there remained a few émigré Europeans scholars who had been part of the diaspora from totalitarian movements that had destroyed Western, Central and

---

1   Catholic philosopher at the University of Dallas from 1965–1996 (http://guardduty.wordpress.com/2007/06/12/frederick-d-wilhelmsen-christendoms-troubadour)

Eastern Europe and Russia. Learning the fundamentals of classi-cal political philosophy from two Protestants and one Catholic priest was clearly an exception in American higher education.

Contrary to what was going on around them at Notre Dame and other American Catholic colleges and universities that were beguiled by the presidency of John F. Kennedy, the Civil Rights movement of Martin Luther King, and the anti-Vietnam war movement, these classical philosophers gave me free reign to un-leash my desire to grow in my studies without impediment by a developing Left University.[2]

Though it is not necessary to state this, contrary to criticism leveled at conservative scholarship by the Left, under their tute-lage I was not learning doctrine, nor becoming a conservative ac-tivist. I was being encouraged to take on the adult responsibility of "existence in truth"[3] of classical philosophy with all my intel-lect.

I am struggling to describe my condition of ignorance, of knowing nothing, yet being aware that I was in the right place to learn everything I had begun to seek as an undergraduate. In try-ing to account for that experience, I have encountered many false starts.

At the beginning of this effort to recall those days in my new "home," I knew it would be very difficult—for me at least—since the works of Eric Voegelin, Gerhart Niemeyer and Fr. Stanley Parry are not suitable for compiling lists of their ideas.

They asked and attempted to answer the great questions of the Western philosophical tradition: "What is order?," "What is right by nature?" "What is tradition?" "What is ideology?" "What is history?" "What is philosophy?" "What is nature?" Thus part of my discovery was to understand why these questions were im-portant and had to be asked. All these and more were subjects of philosophical inquiry under their tutelage. And I had so very

2   James Piereson, "The Left University: How it was born; how it grew; how to overcome it," The Weekly Standard, Vol. 11, Issue 3, October 3, 2005.
3   Eric Voegelin, "On Debate and Existence," p. 36.

much to learn, so many things to read, so many languages to study, and, I thought, so little time.

Rather than begin by attempting to explain the sum of what I learned from Voegelin, Niemeyer and Parry at Notre Dame, let me begin with the curriculum of courses in political theory that I would take with them.

Niemeyer taught a concentrated year-long graduate course titled "Communist Ideology" that required that we read most of the works of Marx and Engels, Lenin, Stalin and Mao Tse-tung, and the major Communist Party pronouncements. Niemeyer also taught two undergraduate courses, one titled "Modern Ideology," in which we read histories of medieval millennialism, the texts of Manicheans and ancient Gnostics, and decadence in literature. That was followed by a course on the recovery of political theory anchored in Voegelin's works, Camus's *The Rebel*, Bergson's *Two Sources of Morality and Religion*, and the studies in comparative religion of Mircea Eliade.

Niemeyer taught two additional seminars with a focus on the concept of nature and the concept of history where we necessarily became absorbed in the basic texts of the major philosophers who had addressed those subjects.

Fr. Stanley Parry taught seminars on the history of political theory, classical and modern, and, in my first semester, I had the opportunity to read St. Augustine and Thomas Hobbes under his tutelage.

Eric Voegelin taught what he wanted to teach under the rubric of Modern Political Theory and Classical Political Theory. I took his seminar on Modern Political Theory, audited his undergraduate political theory class, and attended his lectures on "Revolution" and other subjects. Since Voegelin lived on campus, and dined in the cafeteria, my colleagues and I would join him for dinner and continue discussions we began in class.

That was the substance of my graduate education in political theory at Notre Dame, though I also took a course on Aristotle from Henri Deku, a richly rewarding semester of directed readings in the Presocratics under Ralph McInerny, and a semester of directed reading of Plato's *Gorgias* with Edward Goerner, a student of Leo Strauss. With Goerner I first encountered the intellectual gulf between Eric Voegelin and Leo Strauss. Though I spent a great deal of time analyzing Plato's *Gorgias*, Goerner never uttered a word revealing his own interpretation. One or two other encounters in which Goerner did reveal his views—once immediately after French President De Gaulle's crackdown on student rioters in May 1968 and in a brief discussion about American balance of payments and free markets—gave me reason to question his political judgment. I never took another of Goerner's courses.

Despite that unpleasantness, my research with Ralph McInerny on the early Greek natural philosophers shaped my understanding of the conflict between Homeric myth and the new consciousness of the Greek tragedians and philosophers. And, since I had to demonstrate competence, if not mastery in two other fields of Political Science, I took some courses in Constitutional Law and American Political Theory. That made up the four areas of my Ph.D. examination and oral defense: Greek Philosophy (Ralph McInerny); Political Theory (Gerhart Niemeyer); Constitutional Law (Paul Bartholomew); and American Political Thought (Fr. Raymond Coors). Stephen Tonsor at the University of Michigan was also assigned to read my dissertation. At my dissertation defense, three of four members of my Ph.D. committee were persons on whom I could rely to vote in my favor. Today, unfortunately, it is extremely difficult to find three conservatives in the same graduate department at any American university.[4] Even as few as two conservative scholars cannot be found in the same department in higher education today, and, as a result, it is impossible to assure that conservative graduate students will succeed in earning a Ph.D. During the period of anti-Vietnam war riots on American campuses, if a graduate student or untenured professor spoke out in favor of America's commitment to deter

4   At the University of Virginia, tenure decisions are reviewed by ten scholars. In American higher education, the only way to appease ten reviewers of your candidacy for tenure is to displease no one.

the expansion of Communism, he could be expected to be drummed out of his department's graduate program or have his employment terminated.

As I try to recall my years at the University of Notre Dame, I am struck by events in class, and moments in my readings that enlightened my understanding. Coming to Notre Dame mid-year in the academic calendar, after working in the 1964 Goldwater campaign, I began Niemeyer's course on Communist Ideology midway by reading Lenin without having the benefit of a semester's reading of Marx and Engels. As a result, I found the entire experience less than enjoyable. Actually, I did not do well. As Niemeyer explained, "A grade of 'B' in graduate school is not good."

But, there was Fr. Parry's course that had a focus on St. Augustine and I began then my interest in the wonderful mind of this Catholic saint. I hope that when I die I will have an opportunity to meet this great Christian, and to have the opportunity to continue my education at his feet. Voegelin's seminar on Modern Political Theory was also a challenge since I lacked the tools of classical philosophy. And my language training was deficient. I had to make up what I should have begun in secondary school and college by studying Latin, Classical Greek and German, before completing my Ph.D. dissertation. Later, I added Sanskrit, the language of Hindu religion and the Upanishads.

But, of course, there was much more to the Notre Dame experience.

A more European environment would be difficult to find in the United States than what transpired on a daily basis in South Bend, Indiana. In the Philosophy Department Henri Deku, a German scholar, taught Aristotle; Nickolaus Lobkowicz, a Czech Count, taught Marx; Ralph McInerny taught the Scholasticism of St. Thomas and gave me a chance to read the Presocratics in private tutorials—those were just a few of the scholars with whom I came into contact. I enjoyed every moment, but, until I stepped onto the tarmac at South Bend airport in January, 1965, I had never read a word of the Presocratics, Plato, Aristotle, or St. Augustine. At the University of Pittsburgh my education started with the nineteenth century and ended with behaviorist political science that was the "rage" in higher education in the 1960s.

Though Fr. Stanley Parry's seminar on Thomas Hobbes and St. Augustine was the first and only course that I took with him, a fellow graduate student and I journeyed to Chicago with him to attend meetings of the Philadelphia Society. That gave us the opportunity to spend personal time with him and brought us into close proximity with leaders of a new and exciting conservative "movement." Formed after the 1964 election, the Philadelphia Society attracted all the major personalities we associate with modern conservatism: Frank Meyer, Milton Friedman, Stephen Tonsor, Russell Kirk, Stefan Possony, Thomas Molnar, Willmoore Kendall, Robert Strausz-Hupé, L. Brent Bozell, and Gerhart Niemeyer. Being in the presence of these senior members of the conservative community gave us additional inspiration to join them by completing our postgraduate degree program at Notre Dame. Shortly after that seminar on Hobbes and St. Augustine, Fr. Parry left Notre Dame, experiencing disappointment and betrayal in being removed from his position as Chairman of the Department of Government. He left Notre Dame for Washington, D.C. where he conducted a project for William J. Baroody, Sr., founder of the American Enterprise Institute. His research was to lead to a study of Cong. Howard Smith (D-VA), powerful Chairman of the House Rules Committee. "Judge" Smith, who from 1955 to 1964 blocked passage of civil rights legislation, finally capitulated by releasing President Kennedy's civil rights legislation from the House Rules Committee. Later I asked Fr. Parry what he discovered and he said that Cong. Smith had cleaned his files before he sent them to be archived. Thus the evidence of what actually occurred when he released Kennedy's legislation from the Rules Committee was lost forever. Fr. Parry next taught at the University of Dallas where I had begun my first teaching position as an Assistant Professor of Politics. He was fifty-four years old when he died in 1972. He once told me that the average age of Congregation of Holy Cross priests buried in the cemetery at Notre Dame was fifty-seven.

Dr. John Gueguen's essay in Logos (2007)[5] succinctly examines Fr. Parry's work and influence, gives a close reading of his analysis of Orestes Brownson, and discusses his extraordinary collaboration with Gerhart Niemeyer in 1958 that led to a memorandum, published in Notre Dame's *Scholastic* magazine, suggesting how the U.S. government should address the issue of minority civil rights.

President Eisenhower had created the U.S. Commission on Civil Rights in the fall of 1957 and the Parry/Niemeyer memorandum outlined what can only be called a "conservative" approach to resolving "mutually exclusive concepts of justice."[6] In light of the civil disturbances of the 1960s and 1970s associated with the civil rights movement, the clash between state governments and the federal government, and violence inflicted on demonstrators leading ultimately to the assassination of Martin Luther King in 1968, Parry and Niemeyer were far ahead of events in calling for a "constitutional structure" that assigns to the government

> an all-embracing order of justice and constitutes a concept of the common good acceptable to groups with conflicting notions of justice. In other words, where people hold different and unreconciled ideas about justice, a limited function of the state is a moral duty. The state acts as an instrument of virtue precisely by refraining from acting as an instrument of salvation. It makes possible a peaceful and just community by confining itself to the peacemaking tasks of a reconciling constitutional structure.[7]

5   John A. Gueguen, Jr., "Stanley Parry: Teacher and Prophet," Logos, Vol. 10, No. 2 (Spring 2007).

6   Ibid., p. 7.

7   "Politics and Morality in Civil Rights," The Scholastic, January 17, 1958, p. 12. This issue of the Scholastic may be accessed online at http://www.archives.nd.edu/Scholastic/VOL_0099/VOL_0099_ISSUE_0011.pdf.

The Parry/Niemeyer memorandum argues that it is wrong for a government to "consider itself an instrument for the moral elevation or correction of groups of citizens." But it is right for a government to "take authoritative action to protect the order of justice" by using laws to educate people "to practice forbearance . . . in spite of disagreeing convictions and to subordinate partial interests to the common good."[8]

Fifty-six years after publication of this memorandum, it still amazes me how prescient Parry and Niemeyer were, and what their effort tells us about their own sense of public duty, and their seeming knowledge that they, as representatives of the Government faculty at Notre Dame, spoke with some authority to a willing audience of similarly concerned citizens. In fact, both Parry and Niemeyer had close ties to the Republican Party, the Eisenhower administration and Bill Baroody's "think tank," the American Enterprise Institute, that presaged the relationship between the Hoover administration and the Reagan administration. Between the last year of the Eisenhower administration and the election of President Reagan, everything that Parry and Niemeyer cautioned would occur did occur, and a twenty-year conservative rout removed common sense from American politics. The damage done to American society, culture and basic institutions by an aggressive administrative state during the decades of the '60s and '70s is something that Conservative Rebels are compelled to overcome more than half a century later.

Fr. Parry's essay, "The Restoration of Tradition," published in *Modern Age* in Spring 1961, remains his legacy.

What is tradition is an important problem in science. Parry begins his essay by identifying his subject as "paradigmatic" as opposed to "chronological" tradition. Paradigmatic history is measured by "the integrity of the original compact experience of truth whose differentiation constitutes the stages of the history."[9]

8   Ibid., p. 13.
9   Stanley Parry, "The Restoration of Tradition," *Modern Age* (Spring 1961), p. 126.

Within the context of that meaning, he defines tradition as "nothing more than the concrete experience of truth carried distributively and in common by a multitude whom the experience unites and structures for action in pragmatic history." This tradition is important because it completes us as citizens and as human beings living in society. A "sense of communion" with truth that arises in this social setting is "tradition." He writes, "For above all, tradition exists as the experience of truth." That truth, he finds, is "the common good."

The modern dilemma that Parry addresses in his essay is the descent from truth to falsehood when contemporary events "replace the real experience of truth with unreal images of it."[10] Parry identifies the contest between liberals and conservatives as representative of a change in tradition that "involves a diminution in the intensity of communally experienced truth—in consensus—and a falling out of the area of experience large segments of previously held truth." This type of change "is not a change from one positive position to another, but a change from order and truth to disorder and negation."

Living in a society in which tradition is contested is a hallmark of contemporary America and though we experience discomfort and are ill at ease in daily life, Parry suggests that something more, even dangerous, is at work. In societies that experience a loss of tradition a change from order to disorder occurs that "works itself out as a disruption of the individual soul, a change in which man continues as an objective ontological existent, but no longer as a man." In other words, we move towards a condition of loss of our humanity! Recently a former student told me, "I can no longer recognize my country." That is symptomatic of the dissolution of tradition and the removal of ideas for reform from society "into the isolation of an ideational existence in the minds of unrelated individuals."[11] Ideas now gain importance not as "the form of society" but as "goals of creative

10   Ibid., p. 127.
11   Ibid., p. 131.

action."[12] That is accompanied by an increase in the role of government in imposing those ideas and the absence of "theoretical argument" about their truth.

In seeming anticipation of some contemporary "conservative" responses to our current disorders, Parry suggests that the responses of "economic individualism" and "spiritual individualism" are insufficient. Laissez-faire capitalism's economic response to collectivism is inadequate because it is based solely in economics. And those who identify society itself as the villain will not find a solution in "the realm of the individual's return to truth by paths sometimes solitary and stern."[13]

Parry admits that he himself does not have the answer to our current crisis. Fortunately, he writes, similar crises have occurred at least twice, once during the collapse of the Greek city-state and again at the collapse of the Roman empire. Both generated restorative responses, that of Plato and that of St. Augustine, and each response is prophetic requiring "the attempt to restore tradition to its ontological status as the form of society."[14] The recovery process is made difficult because the criticism brought to the analysis of the disorder will discover that "the principle in which dissolution originates is itself part of the tradition." When and if some semblance of a prophetic response to the crisis appears it "must ultimately express itself as a new interpretation of history itself in which the break, the dissolution, becomes part of a larger pattern of purpose."[15]

My encounter with Gerhart Niemeyer at Notre Dame was life-changing. I first met him in a memorable meeting in his office in January 1965, and throughout that semester I struggled to comprehend the content of the second course in a two-course sequel on Communist Ideology. At the end of that semester, he arranged an internship for me at Georgetown University's Center for

12 Ibid., p. 132.
13 Ibid., p. 134.
14 Ibid., p. 136.
15 Ibid., p. 137.

Strategic Studies with his former student, Richard V. Allen. I returned to Notre Dame in September 1965 and completed Niemeyer's course on History and Political Order and the first part of his seminar on Communist Ideology. In January 1966, feeling deficient in classical Latin and Greece, I took a leave of absence to enroll in a concentrated Latin program at Loyola University of Chicago and a summer introduction to classical Greek at Hunter College. I returned to Notre Dame in Fall 1966 and served two years as Niemeyer's graduate teaching assistant, also completing his seminar on Concepts of Nature. In Fall 1968, I left Notre Dame to attend classes with Michael Oakeshott at the London School of Economics and to work on my Ph.D. dissertation on Thomas Carlyle and nineteenth-century Gnosticism I returned to the United States in Fall 1969 to teach in the Department of Government at Notre Dame. In 1970, Niemeyer visited the University of Dallas where in typical Niemeyer fashion he expressed concern that my dissertation was not on track. Such encounters, few as they were, had an immediate effect. I rectified my errors and completed my Ph.D. dissertation in early 1971.

Niemeyer's biography has been summarized by Walter Nicgorski,[16] Michael Henry,[17] Bruce Fingerhut[18] and others. Bruce Fingerhut's summary outline places Niemeyer's life in historical context:

> Born February 15, 1907, in Essen, Germany, Gerhart Niemeyer was educated at Cambridge (1925–1926),

16 Walter Nicgorski, "Politics, Political Philosophy, and Christian Faith: Gerhart Niemeyer's Journey," in "A Symposium on Gerhart Niemeyer," ed. Michael Henry, The Political Science Reviewer, Vol. XXXI, 2002. This essay may be accessed at **http://www.firstprinciplesjournal.com/articles.aspx ?loc=ja&article=1597**

17 Michael Henry, ed., *The Loss and Recovery of Truth. Selected Writings. Gerhart Niemeyer* (South Bend, IN: St. Augustine's Press, 2013).

18 Bruce Fingerhut, "Look for the Lift: A Biographical Essay of Gerhart Niemeyer," in "A Symposium on Gerhart Niemeyer," ed. Michael Henry, The Political Science Reviewer, Vol. XXXI, 2002. This essay may be accessed at **http://www.firstprinciplesjournal.com/articles.aspx?article=1596**.

Munich (1926–1927) and Kiel (1927–1930), where he received a J.U.D. in 1932. He left Germany in 1933 and joined friend and mentor Hermann Heller in Madrid, Spain. His career as a teacher began as a lecturer at the University of Madrid in 1933–1934, and assistant professor at the Institute for International and Economic Studies in Madrid in 1934–1936. In 1936, he left Madrid for what was to be a brief vacation. A week later the Spanish Civil War erupted, preventing his return to the Institute. He emigrated to the United States in 1937, becoming a citizen in 1943, and began teaching at Princeton (until 1944) and Oglethorpe (1944–1950). He served as visiting professor at Yale (1942, 1946, 1954–1955), Columbia (1952) . . . .

Here the intervention of Fr. Parry in 1955 was critical. Parry's desire to bring Gerhart Niemeyer to the Department of Government at Notre Dame required approval of Notre Dame's president, Fr. Theodore Hesburgh. Parry accumulated letters of recommendation and sent them to the president's office over a series of weeks. Finally, Fr. Hesburgh gave his assent. That assured that Niemeyer's intellectual quest would be based in a supportive institution. No outline of Niemeyer's life, however, can inform those who did not know him of his personal gravitas. In every life men and women may be fortunate once or twice to encounter someone who turns us around or redirects our lives in ways that make all the difference. Gerhart Niemeyer was such a person.

His entry into my life, and the lives of the biographers of Gerhart Niemeyer cited above, begins with his appointment in 1955. The University of Notre Dame is one of several Catholic universities that have made major contributions to American politics, scholarship, religion and science. But Notre Dame, for at least two decades from 1955 to 1975, was unique in that it was open to seminal work in political theory by its Department of Government's Stanley Parry, Gerhart Niemeyer and Eric Voegelin.

Niemeyer and Parry were the anchors that held the accomplishments of these three scholars in a dynamic relationship with their students. I personally mark the fifty years since the removal of Stanley Parry as Chairman of the Department of Government as the commencement of Notre Dame's decline into a secular university. But, for a brief period—more than enough time to launch the careers of many of the political theorists we associate with the recovery of classical political theory in America and the Conservative Rebellion—Notre Dame was the place to study political philosophy. If that statement is true, its truth may be traced to the influence of Gerhart Niemeyer.

My appointment as Niemeyer's teaching assistant was also formative and required that I learn how to grade papers and exams of undergraduate students in his History of Political Theory class. That course was required of Government majors, and I was assigned to teach the 8:00 am section of his class that met on Saturday mornings. Though one might assume that 8:00 am on a Saturday would not attract many students, in fact my class session was full of students who wanted to avoid preparing for the likelihood that Dr. Niemeyer would call on them to explain that week's reading assignment.

Like Fr. Parry, Gerhart Niemeyer's influence did not depend on the books he published, though they include an early work, *Law Without Force* (1941), *An Inquiry into Soviet Mentality* (1956), *The Communist Ideology* (vol. I of *Facts on Communism*, 1959), *Handbook on Communism* (edited with J. M. Bochenski, 1962), *An Outline of Communism* (1966), *Deceitful Peace* (1971), *Between Nothingness and Paradise* (1971), *Aftersight and Foresight* (1988), and *Within and Above Ourselves* (1996).

Niemeyer, like everyone born in the twentieth century, lived in interesting times that shaped his life's work. Faced with the threat of an international communist movement fueled by a Russian nation captured by Bolsheviks, Americans knew little to nothing about communism, the nature of "ideology," and the revolutionary agenda of the Soviet Union. And the ignorance of the United States government in its relations with the Soviet

Union during World War II could easily have ended with the death of freedom in the West. What Americans did know about communism was false, that Stalin was a reformer much like the reformers of the "New Deal." That ignorance led to the beginning of a Cold War. Americans, like the ancient Romans, are a practical people; we are "doers" not "thinkers," and unlike the ancient Greeks, philosophy does not easily come to us. Thus, faced with a regime governed by an ideological program of world domination, it was, simply, too difficult for most Americans to understand the nature of the threat.

Gerhart Niemeyer devoted a significant portion of his professional career to make known to his fellow Americans what the Communist threat was, what its intentions were, and how and why those ideological principles were aimed at the heart of the Christian West. Five of the books in his curriculum vitae are focused on communism. And his students in the graduate program in Government at Notre Dame were initiated into Communist Ideology through an intensive program of required reading of, literally, every work of Marx, Engels, Lenin, Stalin, the Communist Party of the Soviet Union and Mao Tse-tung. How difficult that was for me and many others in Niemeyer's two-semester Communist Ideology course can only be measured by our relief that the Soviet Union collapsed in 1991 and we no longer had to study the ideas of that regime. I must have learned something, however, since the first and only time I taught a course on communist ideology in 1975, I was pleasantly surprised by the interest of my students in learning something about this ideology and how quickly they discerned the threat it presented to our "bourgeois" concepts of freedom. After completing that course, they might be seduced by liberal politicians, but not by communists.

Niemeyer's *Between Nothingness and Paradise* (1971), the collection of his essays published in *Aftersight and Foresight* (1988), and the comprehensive, 669-page collection of essays compiled and edited by Michael Henry in *The Loss and Recovery of Truth. Selected Writings. Gerhart Niemeyer* (2013), are the primary resources for contemporary students who desire to learn something about our teacher, Gerhart Niemeyer. As with Eric Voegelin, it is not possible to summarize Niemeyer's political philosophy in a few paragraphs. Like the important scholars he admired—Eric Voegelin, Henri Bergson, Albert Camus, Mircea Eliade, Hans Jonas, J. L. Talmon, Norman Cohn, Robert Nisbet and many others—Niemeyer was engaged in studying problems in science. The "total critique" of reality that Niemeyer examines in *Between Nothingness and Paradise* leads us to insights into the nature of totalitarianism which, following Camus, he understood is a "metaphysical rebellion."[19] The seduction of the West by totalitarian movements didn't occur overnight, however. There was a "long period of intellectual erosion preceding the advent of the activists." The West was, after a fashion, softened up by humanist intellectuals going back as far as the seventeenth-century Enlightenment thinkers. The analysis of how their interest in civil religion led to development of totalitarian political religions begins with "the denial and destruction of ontological foundations of order."

> The quality that we designate by the word "total" applies to totalitarian movements not because they invade what had until then been a "private" sphere of action, but because they aim beyond mere structural change at the denial and destruction of ontological foundations of order. A totalitarian movement acts in a society as a dissolvent of the *xynon* (Heraclitus), the common awareness of the bonds between political order and the nature of being. Where and insofar as the totalitarian attack is crowned by success, it destroys not merely institutions and powerholders but the transpositive guidance of laws, as well as the order by which families and individual persons live.[20]

19 Gerhart Niemeyer, *Between Nothingness and Paradise* (Baton Rouge: Louisiana State University Press, 1971), p. 143.
20 Ibid., p. 140.

Niemeyer's analysis was supported by personal experience. In "From Europe, With Love," from the collection of Niemeyer essays, *The Loss and Recovery of Truth*, relates an incident in Germany, when the outbreak of the Spanish Civil War blocked his return to Spain, that serves to explain how totalitarian rule destroys personal order.

> One afternoon, while taking a walk, I met a little four-year-old girl who greeted me with "Heil Hitler," and I returned the greeting, "Good afternoon." Back from my walk two hours later, I found my landlady in a state of alarm. The police had been there, inquiring about me and my political orientation. When asked why the inquiry, they said I had failed to use the Nazi salute.[21]

Niemeyer sees "axiological" and "praxiological" aspects of the denial of reality by totalitarian ideology. Axiological denial of reality manifests itself in the speculative assertion of a good opposed to the goodness found in the historical world. "[M]an's historical existence is seen as essentially separated from his true reality."[22] The "truth" of the totalitarian is wholly speculative, grounded in the will and imaginative creation of a future reality, opposed to the present, of the ideologue. The praxiological aspect pulls the norms of an imagined reality into the real world and organizes human action according to the false reality. Following Albert Camus, Niemeyer distinguished between a "total critique of society" and "rebellion," which is directed at specific injustices. The Greek word for being is "on" and Niemeyer describes the total critique as a form of "ontophobia"—fear of being—that he indicates is similar to the ancient Gnostics' obsession with an evil demiurge or God who trapped the divine spark in the man of the material world.

---

21 Gerhart Niemeyer, "From Europe, With Love," in Michael Henry, ed., *The Loss and Recovery of Truth*, p. 8.

22 Niemeyer, *Between Nothingness and Paradise*, p. 141.

This similarity is found in metaphysical discontent, the attribution of evil to the environing world rather than to the human heart, belief in the possibility of salvation from the evil world as a whole, certainty that salvation is to be wrought by human action, and the acceptance of ideological "knowledge" of the method of total change as the message of salvation for mankind.[23]

Here Niemeyer speaks of an antidote to metaphysical rebellion in a "philosophy of limits." The concept is Albert Camus's for whom, "There does exist for man . . . a way of acting and thinking which is possible on the level of moderation to which he belong. . . . Politics is not religion."[24] Niemeyer observes that, "For Camus, this way of acting and thinking consists in rebellion, a negative affirmation in which he sees the establishment of a common human dignity."

Between Nothingness and Paradise ends with three chapters that are offered as an antidote to the totalitarian temptation. Like so many theoretical formulations of great significance—one thinks of Aristotle's few paragraphs on "right by nature" or St. Augustine's distinction between the City of Man and the City of God—Niemeyer's analysis in chapters titled "Past, Future, and Present," "The Ethics of Existence," and "True and False Prophets" are eighty-two pages of compact theoretical reflection about the reality of community, continuity of peoples in history, the origin of community in theophanous experience, and what Niemeyer calls "history as a mode of existence." This mention of "theophany" requires that we attempt to explain what has been obscured by the loss of philosophy or, better said, its replacement with the influence of British empiricism. All that we really know, Locke argued, is based in sense experience.[25] With that one assertion, all

---

23 Ibid., p. 142.
24 Ibid., p. 143.
25 John Locke, An Essay Concerning Human Understanding, II.20.2.

non-material reality was banned from educated conversation. Yet an intelligent observer, William James, as early as 1901 had recovered an understanding that there is a world of "varieties" of "religious experience." Theophany is a religious experience of non-material reality, of the sacred, of something "other," that is not part of the world of immanent things.

Some passages from these eighty-two pages resonate for those of his students who took his seminar on "History and Political Order," or assisted him in his undergraduate History of Political Theory course. In his seminar on History we had fourteen weeks to study some of the works cited here, including Eric Voegelin's *Order and History*, Aristotle's *Nicomachean Ethics*, the books of Exodus, Deuteronomy and Ecclesiastes, St. Augustine's *City of God* and *Confessions*, Mircea Eliade's study of the myth of the eternal return, Manlius Severinus Boethius's *Consolation of Philosophy*, Giambattista Vico's *New Science*, Ibn Khaldun's *Muqaddimah*, and Albert Camus's *The Rebel*.

In Chapter 8, titled "Recovery," I will return to Gerhart Niemeyer's analysis of historical continuity in community and his thoughts on Christianity as the historical form of the West which he outlines in several essays in *The Loss and Recovery of Truth*.

My encounter with Eric Voegelin paralleled the years 1965 to 1980, commencing my first semester at Notre Dame in January, 1965; during a semester that Voegelin was in residence at Notre Dame in 1967; a semester Voegelin spent at the University of Dallas in 1971 and at the Vanderbilt Conference on Gnosticism and Modernity that I organized with John William Corrington and William Havard in 1978. In 1980 I visited Voegelin and his wife one last time while attending a meeting of the Mt. Pelerin Society at Stanford University in Palo Alto. Eric Voegelin died in January 1985.

For many great scholars, teaching is an extension of research and Voegelin would use his classes to expound on subjects about which he was writing at the time. I was fortunate to be in his class when he was writing his essay on immortality, and dealing with the primacy of experience in classic philosophy. This was shortly before publication of Volume IV of *Order and History*, "The Ecumenic Age," and just after publication of *Anamnesis*.

In his graduate classes at the University of Dallas in 1971, which I sometimes attended, Voegelin was asked by his students to read from volume two of *Order and History* those passages dealing with the origin of philosophy in the Presocratics. His students were so enthralled by Voegelin, and hungry for understanding classical philosophy, that they forced Voegelin to take something he had written two decades earlier and use that as the text of his seminar.

So, what was all the fuss? What was Voegelin teaching that instilled awe and inspiration in myself and these students?

His focus on man's experience of reality and, especially, experience of transcendent divine reality and amazement at existence, as well as the recovery of classical philosophy were the essential ingredients of his appeal. The dominant academic approach asserted that all things are relative, neither true nor false, and therefore the wisdom literature that shaped the West was mere opinion.

Voegelin's first three volumes of *Order and History* revealed his "philosophical anthropology," an approach that was deeply historical and analytic that explored the artifacts and textual evidence of ancient cultures by interpreting the symbols by which human communities express their consciousness of order. His first volume in *Order and History*, titled "Israel and Revelation," is a masterful interpretation of the experience of Yahweh's revelation of Himself to the Hebrew clans and Yahweh's Covenant with Israel that differentiated Israel from the cosmological empires of the ancient Near East. My friend John William Corrington[26] told me that he found Volume One of *Order and History*

---

26 John William Corrington (1932–1988) was a novelist, literary critic, scriptwriter for television and motion pictures, legal scholar and attorney, and a philosopher and professor of English. **http://www.centenary.edu/ english/events/corrington**

while browsing the stacks in the library at Tulane University, and when he returned home, Corrington told his wife, "By God, he's done it!" What Voegelin had done in Volume One of *Order and History*, and which excited Corrington upon first reading it, was give scholarly affirmation to Christian faith by identifying and interpreting the symbols that articulated the experience of revelation recorded in the Old Testament. So deeply had relativism and nihilism seeped into American intellectual culture, that Corrington's encounter with Voegelin shocked him. Most of us who were attracted to Voegelin's political philosophy appreciated its compatibility with our Christian faith. For the first time in our intellectual journey, we could explore philosophy without the acid of skepticism, atheism and political religion blocking our philosophical search.

Like most professors, Voegelin used materials in his courses that would later appear in his published works. I encountered his seminal insights in classes he taught at Notre Dame from 1965 to 1968 before they were published. During that period he published *Anamnesis* in 1966[27] and "The Ecumenic Age" in 1974. Some of his lectures developed themes that appeared later in important essays[28] on such topics as "What is Nature"; "What is Right by Nature"; "Reason: The Classic Experience"[29]; "On Debate and Existence"[30]; "Immortality: Experience and Symbol"[31]; 'The Eclipse of Reality"[32]; "The Gospel and Culture"[33]; "Equivalences

27 Eric Voegelin, Anamnesis, in *The Collected Works of Eric Voegelin*, Vol. 6 (Columbia: University of Missouri Press, 2002). Also Gerhart Niemeyer trans. (South Bend: University of Notre Dame, Press 1978).
28 Published Essays: 1966–1985, *The Collected Works of Eric Voegelin*, Vol. 12 (Louisiana State University Press, 1990).
29 Eric Voegelin, "Reason: The Classic Experience," Southern Review, vol. 13, no. 5.
30 On Debate and Existence," Intercollegiate Review, Vol. 3, Number 4–5, March–April, 1967), pp. 143–52.
31 Harvard Theological Review, LX (1967), pp. 235–79.
32 Unpublished essay c. 1969, in *The Collected Works of Eric Voegelin*, Vol. 28 (University of Missouri Press, 1990), pp. 111–62.
33 In Jesus and Man's Hope, Miller and Hadidian, eds. (Pittsburgh Theological Seminary Press, 1971), pp. 59–101.

of Experience and Symbolization in History"[34]; "On Hegel: A Study in Sorcery"[35]; and "On Classical Studies."[36]

Lest I give the impression that Voegelin mostly focused on ancient Israel or Greek philosophy, I should report that he was a fountainhead of insight into contemporary studies that bore on his areas of interest and which dealt with similar problems: Frank Kermode's *Sense of an Ending* that explored man's experience of the limits of existence; Floyd Matson's *The Broken Image. Man, Science and Society*; R. D. Laing's *Divided Self*, which Voegelin referred to in his exploration of the similarity of modern philosophy to schizophrenia; the analysis of "religion" and "faith" by Wilfred Cantwell Smith; William James's examination of religious experience in *Varieties of Religious Experience*, that oddly had nothing to say about Greek philosophic experience; Albert Camus's masterful study of revolution in *L'Homme révolté*; and Michael Oakeshott's classic introduction to Thomas Hobbes's *Leviathan*. And, always, Voegelin would favorably cite Bergson's *Two Sources of Morality and Religion*.

Eric Voegelin's "philosophical anthropology" is based on analysis of the experience of the "open soul." The term "open soul" was coined by Henri Bergson, whose *Two Sources of Morality and Religion* is an examination of the soul which is "open," not self-centered, transparent to the divine in its unwilled erotic movement away from self-love. Men who drew the multitude of mankind after them by their persuasive examples (one thinks of Moses, the prophets of ancient Israel, Confucius, Socrates, Jesus of Nazareth) are representative. Voegelin's philosophical anthropology, then, is an examination of the historical event of the opening of the soul in representative men and the consequences of their consciousness of that movement for our understanding of order in the psyche of man, of history and society. Voegelin writes that "The noetic luminosity of participation in the movement of

34 *The Collected Works of Eric Voegelin*, Vol. 12, pp. 115–71.
35 Studium Generale, XXIV (1971), 335–68.
36 *Modern Age*, Vol. 17, Number 1, Winter 1973, pp. 2–8.

reality did not emerge in the history of mankind before it emerged in the philosophers' own differentiating acts."[37] That emerging truth can take thousands of years to develop as when the Greek natural philosophers began to question the myths that had sustained Hellenic culture since the second millennium.

Voegelin's first classes that I attended were focused on the reality that there is experience, and that the bedrock of experience, what he called "the Ground," cannot be refuted—only interpreted. In other words, reality *is*.

"Why is there something and not nothing?" "Why is something as it is, and not different?" These questions, first expressed by Leibniz in *Principes de la nature et de la grace*,[38] fell upon me as if I had been hit by a load of bricks. Conditioned by the relativism of my former teachers, I failed to understand that the unease I experienced during my undergraduate education was the attraction of my soul to the Ground of reality and that I was being compelled to turn around from the unreality of my professors to reality. I would later read in Voegelin's 1974 essay, "Reason: The Classic Experience": "The unrest in a man's psyche may be luminous enough to understand itself as caused by ignorance concerning the ground and meaning of existence, so that the man will feel an active desire to escape from this state of ignorance . . . and to arrive at knowledge."[39]

The consciousness of the open soul, Voegelin wrote, is structured by noetic and pneumatic theophanies, experiences of divine reality, which make up what can be called the "history of theophany."[40] Voegelin's discussion of a variety of theophanies, therefore, is critical to understanding his recovery of the philosophic quest from the spiritual dead end of the Enlightenment. Voegelin's *Order and History*, for example, and his later essays discussed here, explore the development of symbols of consciousness of

---

37 Eric Voegelin, *Order and History*, Vol. 4, "The Ecumenic Age" (Baton Rouge: Louisiana State University Press, 1974), p. 217.
38 Eric Voegelin, "On Debate and Existence," p. 43.
39 Eric Voegelin, "Reason: The Classic Experience," p. 270.
40 Eric Voegelin, "The Ecumenic Age," p. 252.

theophany. Noetic theophany is an example. Though we often assume that translations of ancient works are sufficient, it helps to know the actual words that were used. "*Nous*" is the Greek word for "mind," but that translation cannot begin to express the depth of meaning conveyed by that word. Voegelin would remark how amazing was the opportunity of Plato and Aristotle to "map" the architecture of the soul, and in that effort "*nous*" was very important.

Nous is the highest capacity of the rational part of the soul and deals with "the highest objects of knowledge."[41] Aristotle sees the noetic contemplation of the divine as the striving to be deathless or immortal, since *nous* is either "divine or the most divine thing in us."[42]

The discovery that the order of the soul is, in effect, the soul's openness to noetic experience is simultaneously the discovery of the soul's movement towards differentiated noetic consciousness. Voegelin writes that reality, as the philosophers came to understand it, "is not a static order of things given to a human observer once for all; it is moving, indeed, in the direction of emergent truth."[43] The "truth" of the philosophers is not a fixed piece of information, "but the event in which the process of reality becomes luminous to itself."[44] This "event" is historical in the sense that consciousness of history is a process shaped by theophanies.

History "is the In-Between where man responds to the divine presence and divine presence evokes the response of man."[45] The "In-Between" defines Voegelin's understanding of philosophy. We human beings are In-Between divine reality and the world of existing things, and our consciousness of order reflects that necessarily limited perspective.

The noetic discovery of the ancient Greeks was not the end of discovery of reality. In Israel and Christianity we have a new

41   Aristotle, *Nicomachean Ethics*, 1177a21.
42   Aristotle, *Nicomachean Ethics*, 1177a16.
43   Eric Voegelin, "The Ecumenic Age," p. 217.
44   Ibid., p. 186.
45   Ibid., p. 242.

event that is expressed in Voegelin's concept of "pneumatic." *Pneuma*, or spirit, is a concept used by Voegelin to distinguish between the philosopher's contemplative act and revelatory experience. The Ground is experienced in both the noetic and pneumatic opening of the soul. Voegelin explains that, "The two modes require two different types of language for their adequate expression. The immediate presence in the movements of the soul requires the revelatory language of consciousness."[46] Voegelin attempts to explain the difference between noetic and pneumatic experience of reality by reference to how divine reality is experienced. The divine is experienced from the direction of the "Beginning" and from the "Beyond." The "Beyond" refers to Plato's symbol of experience of the transcendent Good beyond existence and essence, which compels the soul in its movement away from the world of shadows and ignorance. As such the "Beyond" is a symbol that articulates the experience of divine reality beyond the world of immanent existence. The experience of divine reality from the direction of a "Beginning" is symbolized in the language of cosmogonies which extend in their historical range from the cosmogonic myths of Egypt and Mesopotamia, to the account of creation in Genesis and the formulation of the Gospel of John that "In the beginning was the Word." Though God is revealed beyond the cosmos, "the differentiation of existential truth does not abolish the cosmos in which the event occurs."[47]

Thus, in the Christian experience of the Gospel of John, the "Word" of the "Beginning" is identified with the Word of Christ who manifests the movement of the Word from the Beyond. In this manner, Voegelin identifies the equivalence of the reality experienced in philosophy with the reality experienced in the Gospels and does not accept the conventional opposition between reason and revelation.

Analyzed on the level of experience, noetic theophany articulates an aspect of the same divine reality expressed in the

46   Ibid., p. 63.
47   Ibid., p. 53.

pneumatic symbols of Moses, the prophets, and the Gospels. "Faith in Christ," Voegelin writes, "means responsive participation in the same divine *pneuma* that was active in the Jesus who appeared in the vision [of St. Paul] as the Resurrected."[48] The noetic theophany of Plato is equivalent to the pneumatic theophany of St. Paul with this difference: the pneumatic theophany in the vision of St. Paul is marked by a further differentiation in the eschatological view of the immortality of man. Aristotle's observation that man strives through contemplation to become deathless[49] is given clarity in the Resurrection. Voegelin observes that this is not a matter of "christological dogma." Paul's vision was "an event in metaleptic reality" that "emerges as a symbol from the Metaxy."[50]

The word *metalepsis*, literally translated as "participate," is found in Aristotle's *Metaphysics*[51] and is used extensively by Voegelin to explain that man participates in divine reality and thus is not the divine, but exists in-between. Our consciousness of participation in divine reality is not static.

Henri Bergson observed, for example, that the passage from the closed to the open soul is not an advance of degrees, but a "sudden leap" into a different order of consciousness.[52] In *Order and History*, Voegelin has called this phenomenon a "leap in being"—those historical moments when a new truth about God and, in consequence, a fuller understanding of man and history, is discovered. When a "leap-in-being" occurs,

---

48 Ibid., 242.
49 *Nicomachean Ethics*, 1177a16.
50 Ibid., 243.
51 "And thought thinks on itself because it shares (*metalepsin*) the nature of the object of thought; for it becomes an object of thought in coming into contact with and thinking is objects, so that thought and object of thought are the same." Metaphysica, 1072b19f. Metaphysica, Second Edition, Vol. VIII. *The Works of Aristotle*, W. D. Ross, trans. (Oxford: At the Clarendon Press, 1963).
52 Henri Bergson, *The Two Sources of Morality and Religion*, R. Ashley Audra and Cloudesley Brereton, trans. (Doubleday Anchor, 1935), p. 73.

Not only will the unseemly symbols be rejected, but man will turn away from the world and society as the source of misleading analogy. He will experience a turning around, the Platonic *periagoge,* an inversion or conversion toward the true source of order. And this turning around, this conversion, results in more than an increase in knowledge concerning the order of being; it is a change in the order itself. For the participation in being changes its structure when it becomes emphatically a partnership with God, while the participation in mundane being recedes to second rank. The more perfect attunement to being through conversion is not an increase on the same scale but a qualitative leap. And when this conversion befalls a society, the converted community will experience itself as qualitatively different from all other societies that have not taken the leap.[53]

Such a qualitative spiritual eruption occurred when Israel discovered itself as a community of chosen people, living in the historical present under God. The ancient Israelites were conscious of themselves as having been taken up from among the other cultures whose symbols were expressive of a compact consciousness of participation in being, and made God's special people. In this sense, they constituted a theopolity, or city of God, whose historical traditions began with a revelation of a transcendent God whose love for Israel as a people is visible in the history of ancient Israel. The historical consciousness of Israel did not remain static, but became a stratum of historical consciousness which lay in the background of further development. In the Christian epoch,

When the distinctions are more fully developed, as they were by St. Augustine, the history of Israel will then

53 Eric Voegelin, *Order and History,* Vol. I, "Israel and Revelation" (Louisiana State University Press, 1956), p. 10.

become a phase in the *historia sacra,* in church history, as distinguished from the profane history in which empires rise and fall. Hence, the emphatic partnership with God removes a society from the rank of profane existence and constitutes it as the representative of the *civitas Dei* in historical existence.[54]

Voegelin calls this process of movement, from compact to generalized insight, the process of "differentiation."

Voegelin distinguishes between incomplete and complete breakthroughs or leaps-in-being. In Israel and Hellas, the breaks from the cosmological form were radical and complete, developing in their wake "pneumatic" and "poetic" symbols respectively, which express the character of the theophanies which constituted the "leap." The cosmological civilization of ancient the ancient Greeks was displaced as a consequence of the discovery of philosophy that transformed experience of man as a play-thing of the gods into the source of order of society.

That insight Voegelin called "macroanthropos."

Other societies such as China reveal only a partial or "tentative" breakthrough.[55] The concept of society as "macroanthropos" occurs in China by a "leap-in-being" of the Confucian and Taoist sages, he writes, but the leap "was not radical enough to break the cosmological order completely."[56]

Voegelin's philosophical anthropology goes beyond the traditional limits of political theory, therefore, because political science itself is the outgrowth of a radical "leap-in-being," not a tentative one.

Voegelin saw that the history of order does not reveal an unremitting upward movement towards greater consciousness of being. The experience of the open soul is sometimes deformed. The general term which Voegelin gives to the eclipse of experiential

54   Ibid., 10.
55   Eric Voegelin, "The Ecumenic Age," p. 285.
56   Ibid., p. 299.

symbols is "derailment." Derailment can occur to any symbolism, in any experiential mode. The cosmological symbol of political rule over the "four quarters of the world," analogous to the North-South axis of the cosmos, can become a program for imperial expansion. The Christian differentiation of a "universal mankind under God" can be hypostatized into a quest for world empire. Voegelin writes that, "The possibility of making immanentist nonsense of symbols which express the experience of divine presence in the order of man's existence in society and history is always present."[57] Derailment can take several forms. In the period of transition of Classical philosophy to the speculation of the Stoics, philosophy was deformed into "doctrine." The symbols which Plato and Aristotle created to articulate their experience of reality evoked original experience of the world of existent things and transcendent reality that is not a god but the divine. But once philosophy ceases to be a medium of experience, Voegelin writes, "A new intellectual game with imaginary realities in an imaginary realm of thought, the game of propositional metaphysics, has been opened with world-historic consequences that reach into our own present."[58] The Stoic dogmatization of philosophy, though destructive in its ultimate consequences, had the immediate effect of preserving the insight of classical philosophy against the inevitable defect that philosophy requires "philosophers" if it is to be preserved. In the absence of persons of the rank of Socrates, Plato, and Aristotle to continue the search for truth, and of circumstances conducive to the contemplative life, the dogmatization of philosophy at least preserved the symbols of philosophy. But the ravages of dogmatism can be contained only so long before they take pernicious forms. For Voegelin, the concept of "ideology" represents the final turn in the decline of philosophy when the symbols no longer articulate original experience of theophany, but become the means by which theophany is eradicated from public and personal consciousness.

57   Ibid., p. 148
58   Ibid., p. 43.

Because the creation of ideologies historically occurs later, their construction includes a large arsenal of deformed symbols. For the symbol of the open soul, there is the symbol of the soul closed to divine reality. Voegelin calls this phenomenon "egophany," the creation of a system symbolic of the will of the system builder to explain reality as a function of his own will. The experience of movement of the soul towards the divine becomes, in the work of modern "philosophies of history," the egophanous assertion that history culminates in one's own thought. The Christian mystery of the Second Coming is deformed into egophanous certainty of a secular faith in the this-worldly success of the ideologist's own project for reconstituting reality. The political ideologies of the modern era are formidable not the least because they are deformations of ontologically oriented philosophic symbols of order. In this context, the attempt at recovering classic philosophy is a necessary first step in the recovery of personal and social order in the modern world.

Chapter 4
Living the Rebellion

We post-World War II Conservative Rebels were born into an upside down world of deformed consciousness of order that marked the twentieth century as the bloodiest in the history of the world. World War I unleashed fertile conditions for the political ideologies of Marxism, nationalism, and Wilsonian idealism to assure that war was a permanent condition of life in that era. Entire nations—Russia, Germany, China—became captives of ideologies and exploited their resources to achieve world-immanent utopias. The ideologues motivated to replace reality with better, second realities defined the Soviet Union, Nazi Germany, Communist China and controlled the lives of hundreds of millions of human beings who fell within their power.

In the United States, blessed by distance from these forces of destruction in Europe and Asia, Conservative Rebels came to understand the need to recover our history from the distortions of political religion that had been in development since the American Civil War. Political religion is an ersatz religion, a false construction that intervenes between us and experience of reality. In the United States that reality has been obscured by the general acceptance of a religion of democracy that was developed in America beginning in the 1840s and exploited by President Woodrow Wilson who, in retrospect, can be seen to have shaped how Americans understand what the United States is in terms of a redemptive mission. To state this plainly, America today has the opportunity to recover its originating experience and history much in the way that post-Soviet era Russia is slowly recovering its history after the corruption of communist ideology that dominated Russia during the Soviet era.

Living the Rebellion

From the American Civil War, America's self-interpretation began to be shaped by a civil religion that some can trace to the social contract theorists Hobbes, Locke and Rousseau. Their ideas took root as Americans sought to justify their struggle for independence and were fashioned into a full-blown civil religion of democracy espoused by President Abraham Lincoln. That development has been the subject of criticism by Melvin Bradford,[1] Ernest Lee Tuveson, Richard Gamble, Walter McDougall and others. That their insights are shared by millions of their fellow Americans is visible in the reality of the Conservative Rebellion.

Literally thousands of college-age conservatives, unfortunate to have come of age in the 1960s, participated in what M. Stanton Evans called the *Revolt on the Campus*.[2] This modern Conservative Rebellion, little known, and ignored for years by the cultural Establishment and by the centrists who controlled the Republican Party, contributed to the creation of a political culture that would elect Ronald Reagan to the office of President of the United States. The continuation of our Rebellion today shapes the United States of America through a community of ideas and, for those of us who participated in the Conservative Rebellion, personal ties that go back half a century.[3] Though rebellion engaged us, we Conservative Rebels were concerned with political order, limited government and freedoms that were threatened by the growing power of the modern "state." It didn't make much difference that

1 Bradford, Melvin, "The Heresy of Equality. Bradford Replies to Jaffa," *Modern Age*, Winter 1976, pp. 62–77 and "Dividing the House. The Gnosticism of Lincoln's Political Rhetoric," *Modern Age*, Winter 1979, pp. 10–24. Bradford's "Dividing the House" essay was presented at the Vanderbilt Conference on Gnosticism and Modernity that I organized in 1978 with John William Corrington and William Havard. Bradford's paper was to have appeared in the publication of all the papers given at that conference, but Corrington, Havard and Ellis Sandoz opposed its publication if Bradford's paper was included.
2 Regnery, 1961.
3 Wayne Thorburn, *A Generation Awakes. Young Americans for Freedom and the Creation of the Conservative Movement* (Jameson Books, 2010).

this was an American "state," the whole enterprise was offensive and had to be stopped in its tracks.

This assessment must begin with the collapse of America's founding philosophy of limited government which fell apart from inattention immediately before and around the time that Europe was engulfed in the revolutionary ferment of 1848. Reinterpreted by Abraham Lincoln, who fashioned a civil religion rooted in the Declaration of Independence, it took fifty years from Lincoln's assassination for his interpretation of American democracy to take the form of Woodrow Wilson's international political religion.

The arrival of political religion in American politics is not an insignificant development. There is no lack of scholarship which has identified the religious character of political movements that have disrupted civil society. Norman Cohn's *The Pursuit of the Millennium* (1957), an analysis of medieval European religious movements which is perhaps best known, shows the similarity of these movements to the modern political phenomena of German National Socialism and Communism. These contemporary political ideologies, Cohn shows, are similar in structure to—and in some instances take inspiration from—what we today would call the fanatical, if not irrational, medieval phenomena. J. L. Talmon's *The Origins of Totalitarian Democracy* (1960) indicates the similarity of the secular apocalyptic strain in eighteenth-century French philosophy to the chiliastic medieval phenomena. Talmon also traces the revolutionary consequences of this political Messianism in eighteenth century France. Albert Camus's *The Rebel* (1951) analyzes the variants of rebellion in modern speculation and the spiritual character of revolt. Robert Tucker's *Philosophy and Myth in Karl Marx* (1961) persuasively shows the origins of the thought of Karl Marx in the revolution in religion instituted by German Idealist philosophy's image of man as God. But perhaps most important for analysis of the nature of modern political religions are the works of Eric Voegelin in which he argues that these political movements are essentially Gnostic. These works principally are *The New Science of Politics* (1952) and *Science, Politics and Gnosticism* (1959). Later, Daniel P. Walker, Frances Yates, Peter French and

Stephen McKnight showed the influence of Renaissance Hermeticism in the formation of modern political religion.[4]

Apocalyptic prophets who attempted to make this world into the kingdom of God and assumed that God had appointed or elected them for the deeds which they believed were necessary to save the world were a common feature of the Christian world. In part for that reason, perhaps, St. Augustine rejected the prophecy of the imminence of an actual period of one thousand years in which the Saints would rule the kingdoms of this world with Christ. The affairs of the city of man were not working toward any intramundane conclusion; the rise and fall of nations and empires flowed along no meaningful course, had no history in the theological or philosophical sense; and St. Augustine was no doubt aware of the spiritual consequences for true faith if Christians gave themselves up to the expectation of salvation in this life. If salvation is thought to be intramundane, political life takes on new historical importance as it becomes enveloped in the history of salvation and politics becomes the field of prophecy. Historically, the expectation that reality will be transformed in time is an aspect of the history of prophecy.

Biblical Sources[5]

ISAIAH: The prophet Isaiah advised King Ahaz, then engaged in preparations for an encounter with Syria, not to rely on the army, but on the spirit of Yahweh (Isaiah 31:1–3). When King Ahaz declined the advice offered by Isaiah at the call of Yahweh, and furthermore declined the offer of a sign from Isaiah, Yahweh himself gave Ahaz a sign: the coming of a child, born of a virgin, who would name him Immanuel, and whose coming would be

4 Daniel P. Walker, *Spiritual and Demonic Magic* (1958); Francis Yates, *Giordano Bruno and the Hermetic Tradition* (1964), and *The Rosicrucian Enlightenment* (1972); Peter French, *John Dee, The World of an Elizabethan Magus* (1972); Stephen McKnight, *The Modern Age and the Recovery of Ancient Wisdom* (1991).

5 This review of immanentist apocalyptic sources was originally published in Richard Bishirjian, *The Development of Political Theory* (Dallas: Society for the Study of Traditional Culture, 1978), pp. 186–94.

prefaced by the destruction of the country, brought about by the refusal of the king to reject evil. In Isaiah 11:1–9 another ruler is promised, one who has the spirit of God. "Not by appearance shall he judge, nor by hearsay shall he decide, But he shall judge the poor with justice, and decide aright for the land's afflicted" (11:3–4).[6] "Then the wolf shall be a guest of the lamb, and the leopard shall lie down with the kid; . . . for the earth shall be filled with knowledge of the Lord, as water covers the sea" (11:6–9). The vision of transfigured political life and nature is coupled in Isaiah 2:4 with the prophecy of world peace: "They shall beat their swords into plowshares and their spears into pruning hooks; One nation shall not raise the sword against another, nor shall they train for war again." Passages of similar intensity may be found in the writings of the prophet Jeremiah.[7]

DANIEL: In the Old Testament Book of Daniel, a dream is reported in which a succession of four empires is followed by a fifth which terminates history. The fifth kingdom lasts forever, and governs the entire world. The kingdoms preceding the establishment of the last which is ushered in by "One like a son of man" (7:13) are each governed by beasts. The fourth in the series of beasts wages war against God's chosen people, "the holy ones" (7:21), whom he vanquishes. But God intercedes on the side of the good, and the "holy ones" take dominion (7:22).

> Then the kingship and dominion and majesty of all the kingdoms under the heavens shall be given to the holy people of the Most High, Whose kingdom shall be everlasting: all dominions shall serve and obey him (7:27).

The Daniel Apocalypse was written about 165 B.C., when the Jews in Palestine had come under the Seleucid empire. All Jewish

6   All citations from the Bible are from The New American Bible.
7   For a commentary on the apocalyptic expectations of the Israelite prophets Hosea and Jeremiah, see Eric Voegelin, *Order and History*, Vol. 1 "Israel and Revelation" (Baton Rouge: Louisiana State University Press, 1956), pp. 455–58.

religious observances were forbidden, and this suppression in turn led to the Maccabean revolt. The four beasts referred to the empires of the Babylonians, the Medes, the Persians, and the Greeks. Subsequent generations would associate the four beasts with their own political enemies, whose destruction became a sign of the coming of a new kingdom in which they would reign.

During the Puritan Revolution in England a group of radical Puritans was known as the Fifth Monarchy Men because they expected the imminent replacement of the present regime with a fifth and final one prophesied in the Book of Daniel. In 1653, John Rogers predicted that the Fifth Monarchy would rule the world in the year 1666. Though early Fifth Monarchy Men identified the fourth beast with the reign of Charles I, after Charles' execution when the victorious Puritans under Oliver Cromwell failed to transform existing political and ecclesiastical institutions according to their own principles, Cromwell himself became the "beast." The battle was clear, Englishmen must choose between Christ or Cromwell.[8] Though Cromwell met several times with deputations of Fifth Monarchy Men in order to dispute their interpretations, his appeal to Scripture and political practicality could not dissuade them from opposition, which later became a revolt.

REVELATION: The Book of Revelation also provided a welter of symbols which were to become important aspects of metastatic self-interpretation.[9] In John's vision of "new heavens and a new earth" (21:1), the world is transformed and he sees a "new Jerusalem" which descends from heaven. The "new Jerusalem"

---

8   P. G. Rogers, *The Fifth Monarchy Men* (London: Oxford University Press, 1966), p. 41.
9   The concept "metastasis" and its adjectival derivative "metastatic" were coined by Eric Voegelin to express the nature of the expectation of a radical change in the constitution of being. Voegelin writes, "The constitution of being is what it is, and cannot be affected by human fancies. Hence, the metastatic denial of the order of mundane existence is neither a true proposition in philosophy, nor a program of action that could be executed. The will to transform reality into something which by essence it is not is the rebellion against the nature of things as ordained by God." Eric Voegelin, "Israel and Revelation," p. 453.

is the place where God dwells among men and governs them directly without the mediation of worldly government. In chapter nineteen is described a vision of the champion of God, riding a white horse. His unswerving standard is justice.

> He wore a cloak that had been dipped in blood, and his name was the Word of God. The armies of heaven were behind him riding white horses and dressed in fine linen, pure and white. Out of his mouth came a sharp sword for striking down the nations. He will shepherd them with an iron rod; it is he who will tread out in the winepress the blazing wrath of God the Almighty (19:13–15).

The coming of this heavenly warrior is the beginning of the destruction of the chief representative of evil, which is completed by the binding of Satan for a period of a thousand years (20:2). During this period the saints reign for a millennium in the world with Christ at their head. At the conclusion of the millennium Satan is released to do damage for a short time; then the last judgment occurs and a New Jerusalem is established.

Millenarianism

The socio-religious movements which grew up around the expectation of a this-worldly millennium are sometimes called "Millenarian." Though in its specific sense this term refers to that period one thousand years in advance of the final judgment of man when the saints rule with Christ in a kingdom established in this world, the term is often more broadly construed to define the historical movements which we have called "chiliastic." A specific definition of these movements was made by Norman Cohn, who defines "Millenarian" as referring to movements seeking salvation which is:

(a)   collective, in the sense that it is to be enjoyed by the faithful as a group;

(b)   terrestrial, in the sense that it is to be realized on this earth and not in some otherworldly heaven;

(c)   imminent, in the sense that it is to come both soon and suddenly;

(d)   total, in the sense that it is utterly to transform life on earth, so that the new dispensation will be no mere im provement on the present but perfection itself;

(e)   accomplished by agencies which are consciously regarded as supernatural.[10]

Representative of these "Millenarian" movements are a variety of ecstatic sectaries such as the *pauperes* of the first Crusade, who saw the rescue of Jerusalem as the culmination of the eschatological movement which would result in the establishment of the "New Jerusalem" of the Book of Revelation; the Flagellants, who indulged in self-mutilation which they believed would hasten the establishment of the millennium; and the radical Taborites.

JOACHIM OF FLORA: One representative of intellectual "Millenarianism" was the Calabrian Abbot, Joachim of Flora (c.1135—1202).

Though the prophecy of Joachim was based on scriptural interpretation rather than direct revelation, the revelation of the meaning of history he was to articulate based on the text of Revelation[11] would carry the same authority as more direct

10   Norman Cohn, "Medieval Millenarism: Its Bearing on the Comparative Study of Millenarian Movements," in Sylvia L. Thrupp, ed., *Millennial Dreams in Action* (New York: Schocken Books, 1970), p. 31.

11   English sources on Joachim of Flora include: Marjorie Reeves, *The Influence of Prophecy in the Later Middle Ages. A Study in Joachimism* (Oxford: At The Clarendon Press, 1969); Karl Loewith, *Meaning in History* (Chicago: University of Chicago Press, 1949), pp. 145–49; 208–13; Eric Voegelin, *The New Science of Politics. An Introduction* (Chicago: University of Chicago Press, 1952), 1pp. 110–17; Norman Cohn, *The Pursuit of the Millennium*, pp. 99–103; Morton Bloomfield, "Joachim of Flora: A Critical Survey," XIII, *Traditio* (1957), pp. 249–311. Bloomfield suggests the influence of Joachim on Dante, Mussolini, Hitler, Hegel, and Schelling. Loewith sees the pattern of Joachim's ideas in Lessing, Saint-Simon, Comte, Fichte, Schelling, Hegel, and Nietzsche.

prophecies. The meaning of history he discovered was identified in Joachim's mind with the "ever-lasting gospel" which in Revelation 14:6–7 is carried by an angel who announces the imminence of the Last Judgment. History, Joachim believed, was based on the Trinity. There were three ages, each of which is preceded by a period of slow development culminating in a champion who arises to usher in the new age. The leader of the first age, the Age of the Father, was Abraham. The leader of the second, the Age of the Son, was Christ. The third age, the Age of the Spirit, was yet to come, though Joachim had narrowed down his coming to the year 1260. The leader of the third age would deliver mankind out of Babylon into a condition of spiritual envelopment of the world and mankind. The third age would see the culmination of world history, a time when God would be known directly by all men without the previously necessary mediation of the Church. Men would possess only spiritual bodies and would not require the presence of political institutions. But especially significant was his claim that in the third age the "everlasting gospel" would replace the Old and New Testaments. His prophecies received the early sponsorship of the Church, only to be condemned by the Council of Arles in 1263.

SAVONAROLA: It is impossible here to trace the long history of ecstatic "Millenarianism" which enlivens both Medieval and Renaissance history. Nevertheless, one political-religious chiliast should be noted, Fra Girolamo Savonarola (1452–1498). Savonarola's political activity influenced the life of the first modern political theorist, Niccolo Machiavelli (1469–1527), the Florentine politician and theorist whose own political career began with Savonarola's fall. His teachings were a vital aspect of the life of Florence. His prophecy of a new Cyrus who would lead Florence and all Italy to a condition of unity was met with special acclaim in the city which traditionally believed itself destined to play a special role in history.

Fra Girolamo Savonarola was not a radical hermit but the premier preacher in Renaissance Florence. The men who came to hear his sermons constituted the elite of civic life. Yet he was instrumental in bringing popular government to the city which, by 1494, had been ruled for two generations by the Medici family. Savonarola was brought to Florence at the suggestion of Giovanni Pico della Mirandola, and Savonarola himself saw in this appointment the will of God, who would use him as the means by which to warn all Italy to prepare themselves for the significant events of the immediate future. Savonarola's prophecies of the future contained the typically chiliastic mixture of the promise of spiritual fulfillment and worldly enrichment. Before this condition of reconstituted existence would come about, he predicted that all Italy would first be destroyed.[12] These predictions of doom were not isolated prophecies, but bore the colorings of apocalyptic prophecies with which his hearers would have been abundantly familiar. In Savonarola's "Renovation Sermon" he reveals the contents of a vision he experienced on Good Friday. Over the city of Rome he saw a black cross on which were written the words *"Crux irae Dei,"* "The cross of the wrath of God." The air was filled with tumult, and a battle involving all the peoples of the earth ensued. Then there appeared a golden cross above Jerusalem, so large and bright that it enveloped the entire world with joy and flowers. On this cross was inscribed, *"Crux misericordiae Dei,"* "The cross of the mercy of God." "Quickly all the nations of the earth, men and women, gathered there to adore and to embrace it."[13] The two crosses would signify perhaps the battle with the forces of "Gog and Magog" (Rev. 20:7–9), in which the powers of evil are destroyed before the coming of the New Jerusalem. Savonarola lived in expectation of the Last Days and was troubled by the slowness of God's Coming. He wrote:

> I think, O heavenly king, that your delay, Foretells a still worse scourge for her great sin; Even perhaps that the

---

12   Donald Weinstein, *Savonarola and Florence. Prophecy and Patriotism in the Renaissance* (Princeton: Princeton University Press, 1970), p. 72.
13   Ibid., p. 73.

time begins Which makes Hell tremble—the Final
Day. . . .[14]

When Savonarola was delegated to treat with the invading King
of France in 1494 for acceptable political conditions, he was successful to the extent that Charles VIII withdrew from Florence.
His sermon after the French withdrawal spoke of Florence as the
place chosen by God to illuminate the world with his presence,
and he identified himself as the chosen one of God who would
lead Florence and all Italy from their fallen condition. Savonarola
preached that Florence was soon to become the new Jerusalem[15]
and would become rich both in spirit and in the riches of the
world.[16] Her role in the world was to give leadership to Italy and
to renovate religion throughout the world. In these later sermons
he emphasized the imminence of a new golden age, and not the
tribulations of the Last Days. "His earlier exhortations to reject
the world had given way to the conviction that the world could
be—indeed, would be—transformed, with the regeneration not
only of the individual penitent but of society itself."[17]

Characteristic of all apocalyptic chiliasts, Savonarola relied
upon his own inspiration, his own reading of God's purposes in
the world as he saw them in Scripture or in the events of the day.
With great intensity and absolute sincerity, Savonarola exhorted
his listeners to apocalyptic action. Partly as a consequence of his
coming too close to a rejection of the existing ecclesiastical powers
in his calls for reform (he identified the pope as Antichrist),
Savonarola was excommunicated in 1497, and in 1498 was

14   Ibid., p. 79.
15   Ibid., p. 142.
16   Ibid., p. 143.
17   Ibid., p. 145. A recent manifestation of Millenarianism can be found in the
     Unification Church of the Rev. Sun Myung Moon. "According to 'Divine
     Principle,' Moon's book of revelations, God intended Adam and Eve to
     marry and have perfect children, thereby establishing the Kingdom of
     Heaven on Earth. . . . The time has now come for a Second Christ who will
     finally fulfill God's original plan." Berkeley Rice, "The Pull of Sun Myung
     Moon," *The New York Times Magazine* (May 30, 1976), p. 19.

hanged and burned, after conviction by secular and ecclesiastical tribunals.

MODERN MILLENNIALISM: The metastatic notion that Florence was chosen as the place where God's redemption of the world would commence, an expectation that troubled the political waters of Italy in the late fifteenth century, gave place to the more successful chiliastic expectations of the Puritans of England, who for almost one hundred years from the accession of Queen Elizabeth I in 1558 to the execution of Charles I in 1649 agitated first for reform and ultimately for political dominance. In America, millennial chiliasts saw divine significance in the American Revolution and the American Civil War, out of which would be forged an America committed to the redemption of the world. The epitome of these hopes for America is condensed in Julia Ward Howe's "The Battle Hymn of the Republic," published in February, 1862. It is a poetic, though secularized rendition of the millennial passages of the Book of Revelation: the "glory of the coming of the Lord"; the "trampling out the vintage where the grapes of wrath are stored " (which in the manuscript version more closely approximates the scriptural language, "He is trampling out the wine press . . ."), the personal testimony of the chiliast who attests that she has "seen Him" in the bloody events of the American Civil War and who announces that she can "read a fiery gospel writ in burnished rows of steel." Here is a manifestation of the transformation of Christ's redemptive mission into the social activism of the anti-slavery movement: "With a glory in his bosom that transfigures you and me: As he died to make men holy, let us die to make men free. . . ."[18] Similarly, redemption in the mind of President Woodrow Wilson was the democratic reform of the world. "America," Woodrow Wilson said, "had the infinite privilege of fulfilling her destiny and saving the world."[19]

We should have expected that sometime in our national history, history would be interpreted in redemptive terms.

18   Ernest Lee Tuveson, *Redeemer Nation*, pp. 197–98.
19   Ibid., p. 212.

Experience of the ground of any political order and its articulation in ways that make it effective for everyday practice are similar to the beaches that outline the coasts of continents and nations. The erosion of beaches by the lapping of ocean currents follows a pattern that is familiar to students of Plato's political theory.

Plato understood that all things in this world, including institutions and nations, follow a similar course: an original, engendering experience, that shapes intellectual and political forms; the passing on of those forms at a distance removed from the originating experience; a loss of transparency of those forms to experience of reality, derailment and the possibility of recovery.

Americans engaged in a Conservative Rebellion are living that rebellion in the hope that their actions will lead to the recovery phase of this cycle, and all our skills are now deployed against a nearly fatal derailment.

"Derailment"[20] is Eric Voegelin's concept that he used to explain how reality-oriented consciousness often is "derailed" by those who do not participate or share in the originating experience. Though Voegelin's concept of "derailment" refers to developments in philosophy, the term is apt here in reference to the derailment of America's public philosophy of limited government[21] by Woodrow Wilson's full-blown political religion.

This study uses the analytic skills I learned from Eric Voegelin to explain how nations develop within intellectual forms or paradigms by which they interpret their existence in history. What those paradigms were and are in the self-interpretation of the American nation can be discerned by examining the Conservative Rebellion.

The lessons we Conservative Rebels have learned over the term of development of our rebellion have been squirreled away

20   Eric Voegelin, "Reason. The Classic Experience," Vol. 12, *Collected Works*, pp. 265–91.
21   My introductory essay in *A Public Philosophy Reader* explains the differences between public philosophy, civil religion and political religion. Bishirjian, Richard, *A Public Philosophy Reader* (Arlington House, 1978). Reprinted in *The American Political Tradition and the Nature of Public Philosophy* (Copley, 2004).

in our memories, of which the principal lesson is that a public philosophy can lose its resilience, fail to evoke a response in the body politic, and, virtually overnight, lose its transparency to reality. This analysis is offered as a work of political theory by which I affirm a reality of which I am representative. Much in the way Chesterton affirmed that there was a Victorian age by saying "I am a Victorian," so I affirm that there is a Conservative Rebellion, because I am a Conservative Rebel.

As I write the words "Conservative Rebel," I realize that some claim can be made that a movement of rebellion is, and has been, underway throughout the world since, say, the end of World War II.

Political pollster Arthur Finkelstein has said that his analysis of voting trends shows that the citizens of the United States have been striving, since the presidency of Harry Truman, to reestablish a conservative order of limited government. They were thwarted until 1980. The people of East and Central Europe had been waiting much longer.

The decision of Allied leaders, led by president Franklin Roosevelt, during World War II to consign the peoples of East and Central Europe to the subjugation of the Soviet Union was, in retrospect, a great tragedy. America had the upper hand, and the balance of power was in our favor. We had, as well, the capacity to destroy all opposition in our way. But we chose to allow the communist totalitarianism of Joseph Stalin to mature, to defer responsibility to the United Nations in hopes of establishing a New World Order in which any one nation would be relieved of responsibility for the fate of civilization, and to retrieve American troops from Europe and Asia—post haste.

To those living in East and Central Europe, their abandonment by the West was a sign of the decline of the West, and why the Conservative Rebellion of mid-twentieth century and the hope for recovery of health to the American regime is so important in terms of the survival of this nation, and the civilization of the West in which it participates. Where there is recovery in one portion of Western civilization, may we not hope for recovery of the whole?

President Roosevelt's decision to leave East and Central

Europe stricken with the disease of communism was made not because of a communist conspiracy, but because the fourth paradigm
of Wilsonian idealism contributed to a jumble of misunderstand-
ings about the nature of order, of the threat of totalitarian communism to the order of the West, and a fundamental
misunderstanding about the political and moral obligations of the
United States as leader of the West. The American president whose
crippled body and muddled mind suggested imminent death is,
in many ways, symbolic of the condition of America at the end of
World War II—exhausted from war, economic rationing and the
death of loved ones. Though political theorists can trace this decline from the development of intellectual culture on the European
continent through the Enlightenment to the French Revolution,
American culture had been relatively autonomous of continental
European revolutionary developments—until the Progressive era.

To his credit, Ronald Reagan personally overcame the Progressive ideology characteristic of that era and never forgot what he
learned about totalitarianism, communist infiltration of Holly-
wood, and union thugs. Ronald Reagan was an extraordinary man
and a gifted conservative political leader who intuitively worked
through the political implications of the disorder of the West and
shaped a practical, uniquely American, philosophy of politics.

He well deserves the accolades that have been given to him
in his lifetime. But his time is long past, and as we experience the
events of a new century we conservatives ask what will become
of the Conservative Rebellion?

What happens in the twenty-first century will be determined
to some extent by how we interpret the events that have occurred
since Ronald Reagan left office, principally the collapse of the Soviet Union, the development of an imperial foreign policy by
President George W. Bush, and President Barack Obama's expansion of the administrative state into every aspect of the lives of
American citizens. That means that we Conservative Rebels will
have to focus hard on reality, not the myth of a Reagan "revolution," and pursue an understanding of our current condition with
the skills we learned during the Rebellion.

Chapter 5

Woodrow Wilson, Herbert Croly and the American Civil Religion[1]

Apocalyptic prophets who attempted to make this world into the kingdom of God were a common feature of the early Christian world. In part for that reason, perhaps, St. Augustine rejected the interpretation of the prophecy of the imminence of the millennium as an actual period of one thousand years in which the saints would rule the kingdoms of this world with Christ. The affairs of the city of man were not working toward any intramundane conclusion; the rise and fall of nations and empires flowed along no meaningful course, had no history in the theological or philosophical sense; and St. Augustine was no doubt aware of the spiritual consequences for true faith if Christians gave themselves up to the expectation of salvation in this life. If salvation is thought to be intramundane, political life takes on new historical importance as it becomes enveloped in the history of salvation, and politics becomes the field of prophecy.

Nevertheless, the symbolism of the new Jerusalem (Rev. 21:2), from which God Himself directs human events without the mediation of worldly government; the symbolism of the millennium (Rev. 20:2), that period of one thousand years in advance of the final judgment of man when the saints rule with Christ in a kingdom established in this world; the symbolism of universal world peace when "One nation shall not raise the sword against another. . . ." (Isaiah 2:4); the symbolism of the reconstitution of nature, also

---

1   This chapter was published originally in *Modern Age*, Vol. 23, No. 1 (Winter, 1979), pp. 33–38.

found in Isaiah when he prophesied that a time will come when "the wolf shall be a guest of the lamb, and the leopard shall lie down with the kid . . ." (11:6–9); and the symbolism of Daniel (Chapter Seven) that a fifth monarchy will come which will last forever, and effectively terminate history, are deeply rooted in Western historical consciousness. They are so deeply rooted that the temptation to identify oneself as the efficient cause of these eschatological events has proven irresistible to countless numbers of persons.

Needless to say, examples of political millennialism are not lacking in American history. The titles of two books suggest how our public myths have been colored by the enduring presence of such eschatological religious speculations: Ernest Lee Tuveson's *Redeemer Nation* (1968) and Conrad Cherry's *God's New Israel* (1971). In these works, and in many others, you will find examples of men and women who have seen in our politics and national life signs of the fulfillment and end of history.

Were historical consciousness not the hallmark of Western civilization, we could allow these effusions of secular prophecy to pass without comment. But historical consciousness does define the essence of our understanding of ourselves, our fellow citizens, and the world. The mystery of being in which political community shares, and which its public myths articulate, evokes an experience of history: that the origins of historical political communities are providential; that community exists under the sovereignty of God and serves some purpose; that man, society, and God are participants in a directional movement of being. These are dimensions of the Western concept of history. This view of history past, history present, and history future shapes our identity as persons, as citizens, and as a nation.

We are in possession of a consciousness of history which includes, Gerhart Niemeyer has written, "an irrevocable and eternal past, an informed but yet unknowable hopeful future, [and] a present responsibility before a time transcending God whose will appears in an apodictic law."[2] The present is historical as seen in

2   Gerhart Niemeyer, *Between Nothingness and Paradise*, pp. 173–74.

the movement and openness of the soul to the presence of God. The historical past is "eternal" because the special moments of past time are manifestations of God's presence which have occurred once, left their indelible imprint, and will not occur again. Our consciousness of history also contains an "informed but yet unknowable hopeful future." We find the origins of this eschatological dimension not merely in the promise of God in sacred scripture, but also in Greek philosophy.

Anaximander, the Milesian natural philosopher, wrote: "The origin (arche) of things is the Apeiron. . . . It is necessary for things to perish into that from which they were born; for they pay one another a penalty for their injustice (adikia) according to the ordinance of Time." The mystery of reality was experienced by the classical Greek philosophers as a process in time pointing ultimately towards transfiguration. And Plotinus too wrote: "The One is all things and no one of them; the source [arche) of all things is not all things; and yet it is all things in a transcendent sense—all things to speak, having run back (anedrame) to it: or, more correctly, not all as yet within it, they will be (estai)."

History for men of the West, it seems trite to say, is inescapable; thus when history is de- formed, when historical consciousness is lost and replaced with a derivative, pseudo-interpretation, we can expect the costs in personal and civilizational terms to be substantial. A deformation of history, of course, has occurred. The hope for the future has become a hope dependent on human political action. The expectation of a final end beyond time, at the end of history, has been converted into an expectation of some immanent, this-worldly end, and thus appropriately has been called by Eric Voegelin the immanentization of history, or the eschaton. The experience of the sacredness of national life and its dependence on a higher order of which it is a participant, becomes a certain belief of divine election in which the national life is transformed into the vehicle for saving acts. On this foundation of a deformation of history, a political religion has been fashioned which has shaped the American political experience, has proven its capacity to inspire political loyalty, to rally the nation, and to commit national resources to particular ideological projects.

Consider, for example, the deformation of our concept of "democracy." Irving Kristol has written:

> Once upon a time, in this country the question of democracy was a matter for political philosophy rather than for faith. And the way in which a democratic political philosophy was gradually and inexorably transformed into a democratic faith seems to me to be perhaps the most important problem in American intellectual—and ultimately political history.[3]

Let us follow Kristol's criticisms and the criticism of many others as far as they have taken it. Kristol is persuaded that our civil religion is an attitude of mind carried by a special section or class within Western democratic society, the intellectual class. He believes that the "masses of the people tend to be more 'reasonable,' . . . in their political judgments and political expectations than are our intellectuals." Robert Nisbet has similarly argued that our intellectual class constitutes a "clerisy of power" imbued with a sense of "redemptive passion." The chief vehicle by which they wish to redeem American society is the state, and thus Nisbet believes that it is proper to say that they "have made the political state the temple, so to speak, of their devotion." Michael Novak similarly speaks of the "superculture" and its commitments to the values of modernity—science, technology, industry.

Kristol is also persuaded that the "redemptive" passion of our clerisy of power is a heritage of the millenarian or millennial elements in Western civilization. John Courtney Murray called this "utopianism" a Christian heresy, at the roots of which lies the lust to replace reality as it is given with conditions more acceptable. As such, it constitutes a radical shift of focus from a view of the

---

3   Irving Kristol, *On the Democratic Idea in America* (New York: Harper & Row, 1972), p. 51.

limited state held by the Founding Fathers. Now we have a view of an essentially unlimited state whose function is to provide for the creation of the only real heaven, the one here and now. That this runs contrary to the public philosophy of the Founders who saw that men were limited by their natural tendency to be vicious, and the Founders' fear of an unlimited state, suggests the revolutionary change in attitude accomplished by civil religion in the American context. But it is also revolutionary in a more serious sense. If the state is to become the "kingdom of God," Kristol writes, then any regime which does not approximate the virtues of that city is unacceptable. Only the best regime, from this perspective, is legitimate. Thus the adversary stance by our clerisy of power toward the organic institutions of the American political community, and, we must add, their disillusionment with politics.

Politics requires the adjustment of conflicting interests, and an attitude of mind which seeks the good in the particular. This is an unacceptably dull process to those who seek in politics a field for the actualization of their private millennial visions. Nisbet suggests that the rise of non-party movements and the decline of our political parties is a part of this attitudinal development. To the degree that pragmatic politics is rejected, we also find an all-encompassing politicization of the mind. All problems are now seen to be capable of being resolved by the application of arbitrary power in a good cause, and the grander the scope of involvement of state power, the more hope there is for the realization of utopian visions.

Two persons who represent such extreme eschatological aspirations in the American millennial tradition, persons who left a deep impression on early twentieth-century American intellectual culture, were Herbert Croly and Woodrow Wilson. Herbert Croly's *The Promise of American Life* (1909) and later the journal, The New Republic, which he founded and edited, performed a role in shaping the political attitudes of America's intellectual elite in the Progressive era, a role which Woodrow Wilson complemented by shaping the popular attitudes of Americans towards democracy, the nature of peace, and America's destiny.

In *The Promise of American Life,* Croly wrote: "For better or worse, democracy cannot be disentangled from an aspiration toward human perfectibility, and hence from the adoption of measures looking in the direction of realizing such an aspiration." That aspiration would be realized primarily, he thought, by those "exceptional fellow countrymen" of his, the American intellectuals whom he called "saints." He wrote:

> The common citizen can become something of a saint and something of a hero, not by growing to heroic proportions in his own person, but by the sincere and enthusiastic imitation of heroes and saints, and whether or not he will ever come to such imitation will depend upon the ability of his exceptional fellow countrymen to offer him acceptable examples of heroism and saintliness.[4]

The secular saints who lead the common mass, Croly speculated, will not necessarily be conservators of the American political tradition. The realization of the promise of American life will sometimes require a "partial renunciation" of the American past and of present interests, if necessary to contribute to the "national purpose." There may even occur a sudden transfiguration by "an outburst of enthusiasm." He observed:

> If such a moment ever arrives, it will be partly the creation of some democratic evangelist—some imitator of Jesus who will reveal to men the path whereby they may enter into spiritual possession of their individual and social achievements, and immeasurably increase them by virtue of personal regeneration.

Let us reassemble the parts of Herbert Croly's political religion before examining the political evangelism of Woodrow

---

4   Herbert Croly, *The Promise of American Life* (Bibliotech Press, 2014).

Wilson. Dominating his civil religion is the view of a national purpose to be realized in public affairs. The realization of that purpose requires secular saints, themselves led by a messiah who will reveal the true path. This transfiguration will come because the American nation itself is formed by a democratic ideal which is working its way in time towards full realization. Before this can occur, this democratic ideal, always a promise, must be fully articulated, its creed formulated now, so that the American people may believe once again in the promise of American life.

A critique of Croly's civil religion requires that we return to basics. Politics is a science requiring rational judgments informed by an awareness of circumstances, by a proper assessment of the limits of government and potential abuses of state power, by a concern for institutions which limit power, and by the prudent knowledge of the common good. But Croly's call for secular saints who will conduct us into a condition of reconstituted and transfigured reality, has less to do with political science than with prophecy, enthusiasm, and magic.

The national life is indeed informed by an idea, by public myths which articulate the commonly shared beliefs of society's members. But that idea does not exist independently nor is it working its way in human events towards a logical fulfillment. The national life can expire, change its form, become something altogether different, not by means of the twists and turns of a world spirit, but by the weakening or collapse of civic virtue and of political judgment. How swiftly such a collapse can occur, and how vulnerable the American political system is to such collapse, is visible in the influence of Woodrow Wilson's political religion.

Informing Wilson's political religion is a view of history similar to Croly's. History, Wilson believed, moves according to a plan in which America plays a major role. His view of history is one of a progressive development, moving slowly but inexorably to a condition of reconstituted reality.

In an address in Pittsburgh, Pennsylvania at a Y.M.C.A. celebration on October 24, 1914, he said:

... no man can look at the past of the history of this world without seeing a vision of the future of the history of this world; and when you think of the accumulated moral forces that have made one age better than another age in the progress of mankind, then you can open your eyes to the vision. You can see that age by age, though with a blind struggle in the dust of the road, though often mistaking the path and losing its way in the mire, mankind is yet—sometimes with bloody hands and battered knees—nevertheless struggling step after step up the slow stages to the day when he shall live in the full light which shines upon the uplands, where all the light that illumines mankind shines direct from the face of God.[5]

The role of America in this plan of history, Wilson was persuaded, was shaped and directed by God from the beginning. This, he declared on one occasion, is a nation God built with our hands. To what end, we might ask? In an address before Confederate veterans of the Civil War on June 5, 1917, Wilson declared that, "we are to be an instrument in the hands of God to see that liberty is made secure for mankind."

Wilson's view of history in which America and mankind were moving to a world-immanent transfiguration of the human condition was not an isolated facet of the thought of an otherwise pragmatic man of affairs. Instead, it was an integral aspect of his attitude towards life, and the skills required if political life was to be governed rightly. Politics, for Wilson, required "vision," and vision for Wilson meant knowledge of God's purpose in history. In his First Inaugural, Wilson was speaking of his own visionary politics when he described his task as "no mere task of politics."

5   All citations of Wilson's speeches may be accessed from the "E-Library Search" at the website of The Woodrow Wilson Presidential Library and Museum http://www.woodrowwilson.org/library-archives/wilson-elibrary.

The politics of Woodrow Wilson were not mere politics, they were a special capacity to announce the immanence of a new age certified by the political leader who experienced a special revelation.

Woodrow Wilson's vision of America was one of a nation ordained to play a mighty role in history; it was only fitting, therefore, that Americans should be perceived as different from the rest of the peoples of the world. We, for example, entered World War I "for no selfish advantage." Our troops were "the armies of God." Accordingly, America undertook missions of redemption. At St. Louis, Missouri, September 5, 1919, Wilson observed:

> (America) . . . has said to mankind at her birth: "We have come to redeem the world by giving it liberty and justice." Now we are called upon before the tribunal of mankind to redeem that immortal pledge.

Wilson was an idealist in the sense that T. H. Green[6] defined an idealist as one who seeks to "enact God in the world" by the pursuit of ideals not given in experience. Wilson was committed to the ideal of a world absent of war, a world he believed to be within the grasp of a civilized world. And America's entry into World War I was largely motivated by the desire to attain such an ideal. That it was to be accomplished by violence did not dismay Wilson. It is important to understand that Wilson's desire to involve us in World War I was grounded in his will to destroy the system of balance-of-power politics. Wilson's oft-repeated assertion that America had no selfish interest to be satisfied by her entry into the war, that we sought no territory, no concessions, was his way of expressing utter contempt for balance-of-power politics. On July 10, 1919, in his address to the United States Senate presenting the treaty of peace with Germany, Wilson proclaimed:

6   Richard Bishirjian, "Thomas Hill Green's Political Philosophy," in The Political Science Reviewer, Vol. 4 (Fall 1974), pp. 29–53.

> Every true heart in the world, and every enlightened judgment demanded that, at whatever cost of independent action, every government that took thought for its people or for justice or for ordered freedom would lend itself to a new purpose and utterly destroy the old order of international politics.

Wilson's desire to "utterly destroy" the reality of balance of powers was yoked with his desire to destroy "autocratic authority." He was persuaded that only governments governed by majority rule, not by autocratic minorities, could truly seek peace. As a consequence, he sought to destroy autocratic governments, in the present instance, the government of Kaiser Wilhelm. In such a "good cause" Wilson believed that the maximum use of force was acceptable. Wilson saw a "halo" around the musket over the mantle of the citizen soldier who fought to redeem the world, and around the returning American troops. Force apparently was not to be disdained when executed by the "armies of God." Wilson was in search of a "cause" in which to destroy the existing world order and found it in "the terrible war for democracy and human rights." The war was "terrible" no doubt in part because the winners of the conflict, "the only people in the world who are going to reap the harvest of the future are the people who can entertain ideals, who can follow ideals to the death." But the war would be "terrible" also because Wilson saw the war in apocalyptic terms. This war had eschatological significance. He called the war a "final contest" which would bring about a "final emancipation." And if America did not join the League of Nations he foresaw another "final war"; for surely there would be war again, he said, one that would bring the evil policies of the powers of this world to a close. Looking at history as a progressive movement towards a transfigured condition of peace and justice, Wilson saw himself as living in the last days when heroic acts were necessary to bring history to fruition.

The tragedy of Woodrow Wilson is magnified since it was shared by the people of the United States. His view of history, politics, and peace has become an aspect of America's self- inter-pretation of itself. To the degree that his (and Croly's) view of history has saturated our political consciousness, it can be said that we have experienced a loss of history. Our public past, the history of the collective life of the nation, must express an experience of our participation in the mystery of being or its public myths will become distorted. All Americans will readily admit, for example, that our history has been particularly fortunate. Over the two hundred and thirty nine years 1775 to the occupation of Afghanistan, approximately 848,000 Americans have been killed in combat. That is 216,000 greater than the number of Russians killed during the nine-day siege of Leningrad in World War II. The mystery of why we have been so fortunate should yield the balanced judgment that God's providence cannot be understood completely. From the perspective of Wilson's civil religion, however, Americans are a chosen people, spared the Holocaust for some great event to come in the future which will bring to an end, once and for all, the suffering of all mankind. History is given an *ersatz* interpretation, a pseudo-history is created, and national consciousness is distorted by an arrogance for which, unfortunately, Americans have been too well known.

Woodrow Wilson suffered a disabling stroke towards the end of a national tour in which he attempted to bring pressure upon the Senate to ratify the Covenant of the League of Nations. During those waning days of his tour, days filled with train stops and multiple speeches in American cities, Wilson repeated the theme that over 53,000 Americans died to save the world in a war to end all wars, and that if the Covenant was not ratified by the United States, those men died in vain. Why, he asked, should mothers of sons killed in the war come to see him and speak to him during his trip? After all, he said, he sent them to their deaths.

The visionary politics of a politician for whom politics is a religion, for whom politics is a field in which to attempt to realize an ideal which is not given in reality to be attained is the hallmark of American politics. Recall the following passage from the Inaugural Address of John F. Kennedy:

> Let every nation know, whether it wishes us well or
> ill, that we shall pay any price, bear any burden, meet
> any hardship, support any friend, oppose any foe to as-
> sure the survival and the success of liberty.[7]

The difficulty that this ideal presents has often been com-
mented upon after the toll of deaths of Americans in Vietnam had
been counted. First, it is not the liberty of the American political
community which is to be defended, but liberty in general. Second, our friends are put on notice that they will be judged by the
standards of an ideal liberty evoked by a President of the United
States. Our relationship will be based not on mutual interest, but
on their willingness to impose uniquely American concepts of
civil liberty upon their own societies. Third, it overestimates the
capacity of America to pay "any" price, "any" hardship, and bear
"any" burden. In the economy of real possibilities, such an aspiration is potentially dangerous. It also fosters a cynicism about
politics, because such ideals are never attainable, and vast dislo-
cations in civil society are brought about in the attempt to realize
them. Americans eventually become skeptical of the claims of all
politicians. In turn, some politicians overreact by pursuing a ruth-
less, supposedly "realistic," politics. Policies which seek to maintain a balance of power in world politics, or more immediately
seek to preserve our national interests, have to be promoted
within an idealist framework in order to avoid the rebuke that we
are selfish, and untrue to American tradition. Lastly, the failure
of the symbolism of such policies leads to a general revulsion
against all politics, and the search for the non-politician, the out-
sider, the uncorrupted one, to lead the national life. He in turn
will reassert the idealism of the "true" American tradition, the
pursuit of policies because they are right (to the exclusion of ones
in our national interest). And the cycle of ideological rejection of
political reality begins anew.

7   John F. Kennedy Presidential Library and Museum, www.jfklibrary.org.

Chapter 6
Origins and End of the New World Order[1]

From the revolutionary era's "Spirit of '76"—that "lasted through the failure of the Articles of Confederation, until the Founding of the Constitution of the United States in 1787, and the Ratification Debates in 1789—eighteenth-century American foreign policy involved the prudential act of choosing between real possibilities and their consequences, always framed by an appreciation for the limits of America's resources, trade relations, and a young nation's inability to project power.

In the nineteenth century, from Lincoln's speech at Gettysburg and his Second Inaugural through the expansionist and nascent imperialism nineteenth-century America typified by the presidency of Theodore Roosevelt, a more robust, aggressive, and idea-oriented foreign policy developed. In some ways, nineteenth-century American foreign policy can be seen as an extension of the growth of the power of the state that was the consequence of the American Civil War, America's collective experience in the use of force, and the development of a military hardened by battle that foretold the total war of the twentieth century. The United States had come of age, and was poised to act in such faraway places as the Philippines, Venezuela, Spain and in neighboring Mexico. Still, American foreign policy had an eighteenth-century, classical character as symbolized in this passage from a letter of Theodore Roosevelt to Sir George Trevelyan—"I dread the creation of a revolutionary habit and the creation of a class of people who take to disturbance and destruction as an

1   This chapter is adapted from Richard Bishirjian, "Origins and End of the New World Order," *Modern Age* (Summer 2004), pp. 195–209.

exciting and pleasant business."[2] Nineteenth-century American foreign policy did not have revolutionary motivation and purpose, so much as it represented a willingness to assert American power just because it was there to use. And, the Monroe Doctrine served to remind American leaders that the United States had interests, and that these interests were to be protected. An interest-focused foreign policy was accepted as normal, even patriotic, and is contrasted by Progressive notions that the United States is selfless, disinterested in its particular interests, and motivated by "higher" principles than carefully formulated policies that project, and preserve, American power.

In the twentieth century, Wilsonian idealism redefined American foreign policy. That foreign policy involved a radical change from two hundred years of previous American statecraft, and shaped public views of what the purposes of American foreign policy are. Wilsonian foreign policy views are common among our educated classes, and conflict with the practice of foreign policy by most nation states that are motivated by the pursuit of national interest. The motto of the United States Information Agency, founded after World War II, captured this sense of specialness: "Telling America's Story." This heritage was examined by Frank A. Ninkovich in his seminal work on American cultural diplomacy, *The Diplomacy of Ideas*. Ninkovich traced the role of internationalists like Andrew Carnegie, Elihu Root and Columbia University's president, Nicholas Murray Butler, in framing discussion about the purposes of American foreign policy in terms of international law, and those "'moral influences'. . . as part of the progressive evolution of civilization," that were "gradually, steadily in the course of centuries taking the place of brute force in the control of the affairs of men."[3] An amalgam of Wilsonian messianism, a belief in progress, and the expectation that international agreements will shape a New World Order of eternal

2   H. W. Brands, *TR. The Last Romantic* (Basic Books: New York, 1997), p. 570.
3   Frank A. Ninkovich, *The Diplomacy of Ideas. U.S. Foreign Policy and Cultural Relations* (Cambridge: At the University Press, 1981), p. 10

peace came to define America's foreign policy in the Progressive era, and America's post-war commitment to "Telling America's Story." These ideas became the hallmarks of the administrations of presidents Roosevelt, Truman, Eisenhower, Kennedy, Johnson, Carter, George H. W. Bush, Clinton and George W. Bush, and contributed to the foreign policy failures of those administrations.

It is important, therefore, that we understand the origins of these twentieth-century ideas about foreign policy, their enervating spirit, and their consequences for policy. My argument in *The Conservative Rebellion* that the only truly revolutionary ideology to grip the American nation, and fundamentally reshape America's self-interpretation, was inspired by Woodrow Wilson, Herbert Croly, and Progressive internationalists who championed a New World Order that opposed itself to the old order of balance-of-power politics. The American Revolution was not revolutionary in the sense that modern ideologies that disrupted the world in the twentieth century are revolutionary, but Wilsonian Idealism was. Progressive ideologues like Woodrow Wilson sought a future world—within time—that approximated traditional Christianity's hope for peace eternal in another, heavenly world. And this secular, immanentist ideology successfully challenged the fundamental principles of the American regime, the philosophy of limited government of the Founding Fathers of the Constitution of the United States, transformed the American nation into a "Christ Nation,"[4] and put the American people at risk to even greater ideologies such as Nazism and Marxism. Though the full magnitude of the damage done to American society by so-called "Progressives" has yet to be written, when that story is told it will have significant consequences for American foreign policy. The policy of containment, for example, designed by America's internationalist Establishment in the face of communist imperialism, did not reflect America's true ability to successfully batter the Soviet Union into submission. Containment was not an

4   Richard Gamble, "Savior Nation: Woodrow Wilson and the Gospel of Service," Humanitas, Vol. 14, #1 2001, pp. 4–22.

outward-looking policy, but one that looked inward at tensions in the American mind between our commitment to a selfless, disinterested, foreign policy, and our ignorance of the intellectual and spiritual disorder of modern Western philosophy that degenerated into modern ideologies. In protecting our national interests through containment, America's will to fight was weakened. This intellectual disease of twentieth-century American liberalism cast a pall over American politics until the collapse of the Soviet Union.

If the United States is to survive a new century, therefore, at issue is not whether the Progressives' ideological expectation of eternal peace in history will be realized, but whether, we, American citizens living in this new century, will allow these nineteenth and twentieth-century political religions to shape twenty-first-century American foreign policy and lead the American nation into disaster.

Future generations of Americans must not allow this to happen because if these past ideologies become more fully absorbed into the American soul than they are at present, America will not realize its potential, and may well become a nation quite unlike that envisioned by the Founders of American constitutional government—the instrumentality for a New World Order.

The philosophy of limited government of the Founding Fathers of the Constitution of the United States, of constitutional limits, of federalism, checks and balances and a restricted executive power, constrained by the interests of the nation's representative institutions, will disappear, and this country may become something other than it is now—a revolutionary nation (not unlike the French nation of Napoleon), and a disruptive influence on the world stage, a threat to itself and the stability and order of traditional cultures and world politics. That is the meaning of the title of this chapter, the "Origins and End of the New World Order." If the aspiration for a New World Order is not buried by a more robust and interest-oriented American foreign policy, American limited government, as we know it, may well expire.

The beginning, first, fitful, steps in that journey to becoming a new type of revolutionary, "Redeemer," Nation were taken by Americans responding to the nationalist appeals of Europeans in the 1840s. They had laid the foundations onto which Woodrow Wilson would fashion a redemptive political religion. Because of that, Woodrow Wilson may be ranked as the greatest president of the twentieth century because he created a fourth paradigm that transformed the American regime from a government of constitutional limits treading international waters at peace with itself and other nations, into a new form of government knowing no limits, indeed, a truly revolutionary nation.

In that sense, the New World Order is not a symbol of order, but symptomatic of deep, spiritual, disease and disorder of the American soul. And the aspiration to implement a New World Order by American presidents threatens civil society at home, and promises chaos anywhere in the world that it is deployed. Understanding the basic concepts of the New World Order, and its appeal to American presidents from Woodrow Wilson to George H. W. Bush[5] and George W. Bush is the subject of this criticism of the New World Order.

The mythos of America as a nation justified to act universally because of its redemptive mission has taken root in popular imagination and culture. So deep is this millennial current in American culture that liberals *and* conservatives are attracted by its resonance. But, only Woodrow Wilson was fully conscious that a Redeemer Nation would unleash permanent revolution and that America's historic mission was not to live in peace and isolation, but to revolutionize world politics, destroy the order of balance of power among nations and replace it with a New World Order.

---

5   President George H. W. Bush, in announcing the use of the American military to repulse Saddam Hussein's invasion of Kuwait, "described American objectives not in terms of national interests but in terms of a 'new world order,'" in which "the rule of law, not the law of the jungle, governs the conduct of nations." Much like Roosevelt in 1939, he argued that, "a world in which brutality and lawlessness are allowed to go unchecked isn't the kind of world we're going to want to live in." Quoted by Robert Kagan, "Superpowers Don't Get to Retire," The New Republic, May 26, 2014.

The spirit of the American craftsman of this universalist internationalism, Woodrow Wilson, is kindred in spirit to Karl Marx who called for a revolution in permanence. As such, Wilson and Marx must be given credit for being the most important ideologues of the one-hundred-year period from 1848 to 1948.

By coming to know the similarities of their ideological accomplishments, we may come to understand the origin of the modern religion of a New World Order and the end of reality-oriented politics and policies that previously defined American politics and foreign policy.

The hope for a resolution of the conflicts of existence of this world by human thought and action is a spiritually motivated lust or, to use St. Augustine's concept, *libido dominandi*. The universal hope for peace in God's presence has taken new form, and replaced traditional religious expectations of fulfillment after death with a this-worldly belief that the end sought will occur in time, in this world, in history, not beyond historical life. This displacement of the hope for a transcendent resolution of the conflicts of existence in heaven by an immanent expectation of resolution in time is the most significant sea change in popular culture in American history, and coincides with the decline of Christianity as a way by which Americans live their lives.

The modern universalist internationalism of the New World Order, therefore, must be taken seriously, comprehended for what it is, and its consequences explored, for when a nation is guided by leaders for whom a future international order in time—not at the end of history—is a possible reality, we become, literally, a revolutionary nation. That is what the American nation became during the administration of Woodrow Wilson and his successors.

Understanding the New World Order—as the revolutionary ideology it is—requires that we appreciate what is "new." What is "new" is distinct from Christian faith and the theology of traditional religions.

Wilfred Cantwell Smith makes this distinction in *The Meaning and End of Religion*: ". . . the concern of the religious man is with

God; the concern of the observer is with religion." And, "it is not entirely foolish to suggest that the rise of the concept 'religion' is in some ways correlated with a decline in the practice of religion itself."[6]

The growing popularity of belief in a New World Order could occur only when traditional religion in American culture—Christianity—was in decline. Only the decline of traditional religious faith explains how a modern political religion could successfully vie with the traditional and become *the* interpretation of the American experience.

"Faith . . . is not an entity," Cantwell Smith writes. "It is, rather, the adjectival quality of a person's living in terms of transcendence."[7] Our inquiry into the origins of a New World Order requires that we probe the loss of faith of America's Progressive elites at the turn of the nineteenth century, and their unconscious, and sometimes conscious, rejection of Christianity. That spirit of rejection lies at the heart of this new religion of a New World Order that defined American foreign policy in the twentieth century. During that century, Americans completed the construction of a full-blown administrative state. At the beginning of the twentieth century, the private sector dominated. At its end, the public sector in full panoply dominates every aspect of American life and threatens to spread the viruses of nineteenth and twentieth century political religion by asserting the prerogatives of the nation state.

In many ways, the spirit of the New World Order in America is a mix of socialist economics, Enlightenment notions of rationality, and very deep and rich traditions of medieval millennialism that were carried to America by Protestant preachers, topped off by revolutionary hypostasis of American ideals that, Richard Gamble writes, made America into a "permanently revolutionary

---

6   Wilfred Cantwell Smith, *The Meaning and End of Religion* (New York: Macmillan, 1962), New American Library edition, 1964, p. 22.
7   Wilfred Cantwell Smith, *Faith and Belief: The Difference Between Them* (Oxford, 1998).

nation."[8] Gamble calls the outcome of this development the "Christ-Nation," a symbol by which "Wilson reassigned the divine attributes of Christ to the American nation: the U.S. was the Mediator, the light of the world, the peacemaker, the bringer of salvation." In that concept, Gamble writes, we see "the worst of disordered loves."

Richard Kennington's essay, "René Descartes,"[9] is also important because it places these phenomena in another context—the context of the Enlightenment: "The classic tradition appeared to [Descartes] . . . as a corruption of the wisdom of the golden youth of the world in some pre-Socratic *siècle sage*." "It was necessary for Descartes, following Bacon, to 'enlighten" society. . . ." Kennington sees three meanings of the concept "Enlightenment" in the context of conscious rejection of classical philosophy—what we may call the "political program" implicit in modern philosophy. Kennington writes that ". . . Enlightenment rhetoric has a permanently divisive social function" that encourages modern man to engage in the mastery of nature; advance science and communication between scientist, and promote "open" societies versus those that "seek the autonomous cultivation and preservation of their own morality and way of life."

This "permanently divisive social function" of modern, Enlightenment, philosophy found fertile soil in the shaping of Woodrow Wilson's successful challenge of traditional religion even as he borrowed from the language of Biblical Christianity. The "permanently divisive social function" of Enlightenment rationality accounts also for the wariness, and fear, with which Islamic and Christian fundamentalists view contemporary America today. To add insult to injury, Puritanism was converted by progressive thinkers to secular ideological purposes, and became a part of the fabric of America as a permanently revolutionary "Christ-Nation."

8   Richard Gamble, *Savior Nation*, pp. 4–22.
9   Richard Kennington, "Rene Descartes," in *Leo Strauss and Joseph Cropsey, History of Political Philosophy* (Rand McNally, 1969), pp. 379¾495.

Key Biblical passages, cited in Chapter 2, have shaped America's political religion. They include Isaiah's prophecy of a reconstituted nature, "when the wolf shall lie down with the kid"; Isaiah's expectation of universal world peace, "when one nation shall not raise the sword against another"; the Book of Daniel's prophecy of a "fifth monarchy" that concludes history; and the Book of Revelation's "new Jerusalem" where God dwells among men and governs them directly without the mediation of worldly government.

With the growing social and political dominance of the Progressive movement came a reworking of modern political thought and old-time religion into a powerful rhetoric for national self-realization. Woodrow Wilson's language had great resonance for Americans of the early twentieth century for whom the language of the Bible was their common language. Yet, Wilson was not addressing the aspirations of Christian believers who expected a resolution of the conflicts of existence beyond the world, at the end of history. Wilson was a "modern" in the sense that to be modern means to focus your aspirations on life in this world, not the next, and like his contemporaries, Marx and Lenin, Wilson was prepared to achieve a New World Order by revolutionary action. The similarity between Lenin and Wilson is little appreciated, but both accepted Marx's concept of "Revolution in Permanence."

Gerhart Niemeyer observed that Lenin saw that "history subdivides, not into successive worlds of social order, but into successive stages of revolution. The revolution is the continuum, the ongoing reality that makes a concept of history possible. . . . In each of the successive phases [of revolution], a peculiar strategic situation confronts the revolutionary forces, so that to every phase corresponds a temporary revolutionary program."[10]

The struggle between the fourth and fifth paradigms is clearly made difficult by the hypostatization of the rights and equality that define America today. Those traditional ideas of liberty and equality, when hypostatized—spun off from the context of the

---

10 Gerhart Niemeyer, *Between Nothingness and Paradise*, pp. 115–16.

rule of law, federalism, and historical experience embedded in a written Constitution—make the American people an easy target for those who would appeal to American idealism and ask Americans to pay in treasure and blood in order to impose hypostatized liberty and equality upon an unsuspecting world. The contest, as drawn, involves a choice that American leaders, and the American public, must make: to pursue American national interests, or to pursue "revolution in permanence" through the pursuit of an internationalist World Order.

After the attack on the World Trade Towers on September 11, 2001, American foreign policy focused on putting down the threat of terrorism from Islamic fundamentalists who had captured the government of Afghanistan. The Taliban regime was dispersed, and the administration of George W. Bush then focused on nation-building in Afghanistan and a War on Terror that led to an invasion of Iraq. The decision to invade Iraq had disastrous consequences that might have been avoided if Bush administration policy makers had heeded these five principles of a foreign policy based on the national interest.

I. The political religion of the New World Order is a twentieth-century ideology.

Though this ideology still resonates with environmental activists, and appears in the language of ill-educated elected leaders and the detritus of Eurotrash culture, Wilsonian internationalism always runs aground on reality. Wars are costly, and the American people pay for war with high taxes and blood. After a while, they vote out of office internationalists and policies not driven by national interest.

All aspirations for a New World Order run aground on the bedrock of national interest. Though internationalist rhetorical cant clutters our intellectual journals, academic fora and media discourse with ideological concepts in conflict with national interest, the practice of statecraft and the pursuit of national interest ultimately prevails. Still, the process takes time. So deeply rooted are the internationalist aspirations of our intellectual classes, after a century of intellectual brainwashing, hypostatized ideas of democracy absent the rule of law; equality absent a consciousness of justice; and liberty absent a sense of responsibility, have become the common language of our politically correct elites. In the light of those hypostatized ideas, historical communities must be judged to be defective, including our own nation.

A good deal of the rejection and loathing of politics by our educated classes is due to an underlying sense that the entire enterprise is corrupt, false, and incompatible with aspirations for a New World Order. The New World Order has become "the" American political tradition, and American constitutionalism and an interest-oriented foreign policy rejected. Conflicted by idealism posing as statecraft, the American people have become skeptical. The ideology of a revolution in permanence breeds skepticism which, in turn, leads to a vicious realism absent of virtue. In a public arena filled with unrealizable ideals now perceived as lies, American politics yields the likes of Lyndon Baines Johnson, Richard Nixon, Henry Kissinger, and others, for whom amorality provides respite from falsehood, and in reaction to the acid of that skepticism, the American electorate coughs up personages such as John F. Kennedy and George W. Bush, whose foreign policies constitute a vicious idealism absent of prudence.

The first, and foremost, vicious idealist was Woodrow Wilson. In that, however, there is some hope because Wilson himself is dead. Though dead, he created an ideological mold that was not broken upon his death, and the death in combat of 53,000 thousand Americans in European trenches of World War I. Since World War II, as a result, American politics has felt the needs of a reality-based foreign policy only to respond to appeals for a New World Order. When those shifts occur, they set the American nation on a course of spiritual and political tragedy, death, and war weariness.

II. Universal peace is not a real possibility.

St. Augustine's *City of God* should be required reading for every educated American because it teaches us about true realism, quite different from the flawed vision of the Nixons and Kissingers of American politics. For a man who is sometimes accused of being so other-worldly that he has little to say about pragmatic political reality, St. Augustine's observations on peace are eminently practical. His civilization had collapsed, Christianity was held accountable for the collapse, and Augustine attempted to rally his fellow Christians to a consciousness of the community of the City of God.

The peace of the City of God is what you would expect of a community of men who love God. Their souls turned to God, they look forward with hope (while in the pilgrim condition of this life) toward a life of eternal peace after death. In contrast, the peace of this world is fragile, easily broken, and often more cruel than war. Will there be a moment in time, perhaps for a thousand years, when men will live in peace? No, St. Augustine writes. The millennium cannot be taken literally. It is but a metaphor for the age initiated with the coming of Christ that will end only with his Second Coming.

Contrast those words with the millennial visions of the New World Order, and the utopian notion that nations will turn swords into plow shares which has captivated American elites for two centuries.

What is the engendering experience of this hope? Is it a lust for immortality? Since wars are not desired by reasonable men, and a world absent of war, a New World Order from which war has been banished, is not expected by reasonable men, an element of irrationality has entered intellectual culture and has become socially dominant. Seen in this context, the New World Order should be understood as the prototype of the "modern" rejection of the reality of our mortality and the injection of irrationality in the American soul.

Rejection of mortality, however, is only one aspect of a panoply of modern rejections of reality including rejection of gender differences (feminism and homosexuality), rejection of aging through plastic surgery; rejection of the human tendency to do unhealthy things such as the prohibition of alcohol and smoking, and in attempts to prepare for life after death through quick-freezing. All these "New Age" nostrums are parts of a greater scheme of spiritual disorder.

III. The rule of law, political rights, and constitutional government are the antipodes of egalitarianism, universal rights and the will to impose plebiscitary democracy on non-Western cultures.

America must preserve its commitment to justice and respect for human rights, but that commitment must be based on an articulated theory of justice, and political philosophy.

The account of Creation in the first chapter of Genesis speaks of equality that is rooted in reality. The Elohim, having decided to make man "in our image" (Gen. 1:26) gives rise to the recognition that all men have an obligation to treat their fellow men with justice—as a moral obligation. Every man should be treated equally with the justice required of beings made in the image of God. But recognizing our obligation to be just is one thing. Dedicating our foreign policy to the imposition of American concepts of human rights and democracy on other countries is another.

Our guide should be Aristotle, who tried valiantly to confront the Sophistic notion that *nomos* (law) and *physis* (nature) were opposed. The Sophists, in the late stage of their development, had become moral relativists, and argued that the laws establish principles of right or justice that have as their purpose to keep down the strong. So the natural strength of the stronger, which of right should prevail, is opposed by the laws of the weaker, though numerically larger community of men, who fear the strong. Justice, really, the Sophists argued, is the will of the stronger.

Aristotle's answer, no more than two pages of his life's work, is one of the most significant contributions to the corpus of Western political theory, and a theory of justice that has ennobled Western civilization through the principle of "natural law."

There is *dike* (right), Aristotle wrote, by convention. But there is also *physie dikaion* (right by nature). Justice exists by law, and by nature. Yet because what is right by nature everywhere has the same force, and because it nevertheless changes, it requires the judgment of just men to know which is which. The just man is the measure by which what is right by nature can be known. Right requires judgment, not definition.[11] Here is stated a truth on which stability and order of all societies is grounded—the education of men for citizenship, and the just life. Societies are just that present no conflict between being good men and good citizens. This is a very simple measure by which to distinguish traditional cultures from aberrations deformed by modern ideologies.

Advocates of a New World Order are not guided by this truth. Instead, they are motivated to establish a world in which force has been banished, a world where nations may not seek their own national self-interest, and a world in which supranational organizations determine when force may be used. In fostering this myth, they absolve nations and human actors from making judgments about right, wrong, justice, and injustice, peace and war. And they ignore that there is an economy of justice by which statesmen judge whether to shed blood, or not. That economy was ignored by Woodrow Wilson when, in the name of peace, he created an imbalance of power into which Lenin, Stalin, Hitler, Mussolini stepped.

IV. Underlying the constant imposition of hypostatized concepts of liberty, democracy, and peace on other countries is a complex of secular messianism, moral arrogance, and a profound ignorance of political philosophy.

Self-government, from the Wilsonian perspective, is better than good government. Independence is better than ordered society. Self-determination thus becomes the supreme political good, and for its sake we are prepared to accept brutality. Though quite silly when looked at from some distance, the arrogance of utopian democracy is dangerous precisely because, like someone "not quite right," it is addled. The complex network of social

11   Aristotle, *Nicomachean Ethics*, 1134b16–1135a5.

interrelationships in non-Western countries is such that to impose a democratic paradigm on these subcultures is to do no more than superimpose an ideological overlay that will be fragile at best. The substance of traditional religious, social and political order is disoriented as a result, and what order existed previously may now cease to be viable, leaving only the ideological rhetoric of democracy in which no one believes. That is the dilemma facing the United States in Iraq, and any other parts of the world into which American power may be projected. Once an American order is established, will it destroy traditional order? Will the virus of Enlightenment rationality carried by our academic, po-litically correct, elites be unleashed in a fit of "nation building" so destructive to traditional cultures that future generations of Americans will die as a consequence?

The truth must be stated: It is not in our interest in the long term to impose our ideas on others, because, ultimately, American boys will pay the price in blood, if we persist. The feminization of the American military, the choice of female ambassadors for countries whose women are second-class citizens, the flaunting of our "right" to choose our sexual preferences, and other reflec-tions of our cultural crackup can only lead to failed foreign policy. Instead we should take inspiration from the Founding Fathers of the American republic who saw that the rule of law, of constitu-tional practice, and checks and balances on the power of govern-ment were necessary to balance the demands of freedom and order.

IV. And, then, there is the willingness of internationalists to forget justice at home. The New World Order was pursued by Woodrow Wilson without reference to domestic justice.

Ideologies are not rooted in a profound sense of concern, and pursuit of justice and truth. Western ideological system builders always subsume ethics to "history." Woodrow Wilson presided over the establishment of Jim Crow laws, and was indifferent to the plight of African-Americans. Disenfranchisement of blacks met with no response by Woodrow Wilson. "Jim Crow laws multiplied rapidly. Begun tentatively in the 1880s and accepted by the Supreme Court in 1896, legal segregation moved inexorably forward during the Progressive Era in state after state."[12] The New World Order of Woodrow Wilson was blind to civil rights of racial minorities because it is not based in a political philosophy concerned about order of the soul and of society. Justice plays no role in the revolution in permanence.

The link between those who favor increasing the power of the national government and those who advocate internationalism transcending American interests in foreign policy is indelible. That indelible commitment to an internationalist foreign policy and the growth of the administrative state is linked to the amendment of the Constitution of the United States by Progressives to provide for direct election of United States Senators. When that amendment was adopted, the great sucking sound that was heard throughout the body politic emanated from the escape of power from local governments, and state legislatures, into the federal government. At last, an institution of the federal government could be turned to the advancement of causes unmediated by non-ideologically driven motives, by "interests." If one examines the ideological conflicts that tore American society apart and drove American national politics in the twentieth century, it will be seen that virtually all are rooted in the Progressives' politicization of the electoral process through the direct election of the United States Senate. By that means, the United States Senate became the playground of elected officials who hitched their political careers to ideological "causes" and state governments ceased to be the focus of most ambitious politicians. The Founding Fathers expected the Senate of the United States to represent state interests, not ideologies. The Progressives arrogantly asserted that the Founding Fathers were wrong, and changed the nature of American politics and the composition of the Senate through the direct election of its members.

12   Thomas K, McGraw, "The Progressive Legacy," in Lewis L. Gould, ed., *The Progressive Era* (Syracuse, 1974).

Though repeal of that Amendment for some may hold the promise of a stable interest-oriented American foreign policy, there are deep spiritual forces in the American soul that easily ignite enthusiasms for foreign conquests. That spiritual disorder cannot be remedied by changing procedures.

Chapter 7
Leo Strauss, Natural Right and American Political Religion

Two political theorists whose works define the recovery of classical political theory in the twentieth century were Eric Voegelin and Leo Strauss. Virtually at the same moment when the Progressive movement was about to be given new life in American politics, Leo Strauss at the University of Chicago and Eric Voegelin at Louisiana State University and at Notre Dame were introducing motivated students to the mastery of classical Greek political philosophy. Their students had sought them out because they were disposed to reject the "value free" social science that dominated American political science, and because many saw themselves as conservative" and believed Strauss's and Voegelin's works represented a conservative political philosophy. More important, some had worked on Sen. Barry Goldwater's presidential campaign and hoped that the conservative movement he started would outlive his defeat in the disastrous election of 1964. Many would become politically influential in American presidential administrations as political appointees.

Both Voegelin and Strauss carefully analyzed and rejected the fact/value approach of modern political "science"; Strauss for its rejection of natural right that led, he argued, to nihilism, and Voegelin for its rejection of our ability to know truth in the use of such terms as "value judgments." "[N]either classic nor Christian ethics and politics contain "value judgments," Voegelin wrote in the *The New Science of Politics*, "but elaborate, empirically and critically, the problems of order which derive from philosophical anthropology as part of a general ontology."[1]

Their criticism of "value-free" social science gave Strauss's and Voegelin's students critical tools with which to understand why they had intuitively rejected the dominant behavioral approach of American political science. A few years later, when Berkeley, Columbia, and other major universities were convulsed by student demonstrators, a similar complaint was expressed by campus radicals that "value-free" social science was irrelevant. A post-World War II generation of young Americans on the political right and left were similarly motivated to reject a dominant American ideology. How they went about the rejection of value-free social science influenced American political life in the twentieth century. Students of Voegelin and Strauss chose classical scholarship. Their radical opposites chose the streets. Unlike their fathers' World War II generation, the post-World War II generation didn't accept the platitudes and falsehoods that passed for political wisdom in mid-twentieth-century America. Both, in their own way, were searching for truth.

Strauss's understanding that the questioning act of philosophy is an ascent to truth[2] and Voegelin's definition of a philosopher as "the representative of a new truth in rivalry with the truth represented by society"[3] evoked a responsive chord in the hearts and minds of their students.

Though Strauss and Voegelin addressed many of the same subjects, their approaches were dissimilar. Voegelin wrote on "problems in science, not on topics,"[4] which included the differences yet similarities of reason and revelation, Christianity's radical de-divinization of the world, and the nature of representation

1   Eric Voegelin, *The New Science of Politics*, pp. 11–12.
2   Leo Strauss, *Natural Right and History* (Chicago: University of Chicago Press, 1953), p. 124. Subsequent references to this book will be parenthetically in the text.
3   Eric Voegelin, *The New Science of Politics*, p, 70. See also p. 59–60.
4   Letter, Eric Voegelin to Richard Bishirjian, 20 July 1977.

"as the form by which a political society gains existence for action in history."[5]

In comparing Strauss with Voegelin, we observe that Strauss was more literally "classical" in the sense that his method of textual analysis worked within and with the concepts of his subjects. Thus Strauss's examination of tyranny and tyrants, classical virtue, reason and revelation are rooted in the texts of the great classical philosophers, while Voegelin's analysis of totalitarianism drew upon what he called the "Gnostic" speculation of Joachim of Flora and, later, what he would call "Second Realities."[6]

Both accepted "virtue" as morally valid and true, but Voegelin's emphasis upon experience of transcendent divine reality vs. Strauss's emphasis on reason—the former is all encompassing, the latter rooted in classical Greek philosophy "before Christianity"—is a difference of kind, not of degree.

Both understood that "transcendence," as Strauss observed, "is implied in the meaning of political philosophy's quest for the natural or best political order" (*Natural Right* 15.) The Greek natural philosophers (*physiologoi*) were motivated in a philosophical quest for the origin (*genesis*) of existent things (*ta onta*). That led to the judgment that the origin of nature (*physis*) was transcendent reality (*to on*) that is divine (*to theion*). The quest for the genesis of nature led Socrates to call the moon a stone and to reject the ancient cosmological concept of man as a plaything of gods who were, literally, the cosmos. The work of the natural philosophers enabled Plato to engage in dialogue in quest of the best regime and to outline a history of political forms commencing in a regime of the best men that declined ultimately into democracy and then tyranny. Strauss, working within classical terminology, believed that Plato's and Aristotle's analysis of tyranny, used with skill, was sufficient to reveal the depravity of Stalin or Hitler.

5   Eric Voegelin, *The New Science of Politics*, p. 1.
6   Eric Voegelin, *On Debate and Existence*, p. 51. Voegelin translated the term "another reality" in Robert Musil's *A Man Without Qualities* into English as "second reality."

Voegelin agreed, in part, but saw in modern totalitarian ideologies serious spiritual disorders that could not be explained solely in Platonic or Aristotelian terms. Those disorders were equivalent to the alienation of the post-Christian Gnostics, Voegelin argued in *The New Science of Politics,* and later came to see them related to the decline of Christianity evident in the Elizabethan revival of sorcery and magic. Underlying these totalitarian movements was a *libido dominandi* that sought to replace reality with "Second Realities."

Voegelin saw modern ideologies as distortions of Christian theological truth. Strauss was reluctant, or not interested, in using theological tools in the assessment of problems of political order. Allan Bloom explained this by observing that Strauss "found that the teachings of reason are wholly different from and incompatible with those of revelation and that neither side could completely refute the claims of the other but that a choice had to be made."[7]

By contrast, Voegelin's classical scholarship emphasized the experience of ever-changing immanent reality and experience of an unchanging transcendent divine reality, which enabled classical Greek philosophers to achieve what Voegelin called a "leap in being." When such a leap occurs, Voegelin writes:

> Not only will the unseemly symbols be rejected, but man will turn away from the world and society as the source of misleading analogy. He will experience a turning around, the Platonic periagoge, an inversion or conversion toward the true source of order. And this turning around, this conversion, results in more than an increase in knowledge concerning the order of being; it is a change in the order itself. For the participation in being changes its structure when it becomes emphatically a partnership with God, while the participation in mundane being recedes to second rank. The more

---

7   Allan Bloom, "Leo Strauss," *Political Theory* 2, No. 4 (November 1974), p. 381.

perfect attunement to being through conversion is not an increase on the same scale but a qualitative leap. And when this conversion befalls a society, the converted community will experience itself as qualitatively different from all other societies that have not taken the leap.[8]

Strauss's decision to rely solely on reason implied a rejection of revelation, or, at least, in the light of reason, its incomprehensibility. That seriously limited what ultimately became known as the "Straussian school" of political theory. The word "School" is, in some ways, an apt description of Strauss's approach and resonates with the meaning of that term as it is used to describe the Scholasticism of the medieval "Schoolmen."

As a scholar of classical Greek philosophy, Strauss's consistent use of the term "natural right" raises this question: Why not speak in the terms Aristotle used—"right by nature"?[9] In only two sentences in *Natural Right and History* does Strauss use the classic phrase. "What is by nature right," he observes, "can find its complete answer only in the conversation about the best regime" and "reason determines what is by nature right" (144, 7). This differentiates Strauss's approach to his subject from Eric Voegelin's. Strauss's choice of the word "doctrine" to define his subject suggests that his *Natural Right and History* is concerned with the development of a doctrine of "natural right" and not Aristotle's examination of "what is right by nature." That may explain why Strauss argued that a continuum exists between the ancient Greek philosophers and modern natural right theorists. There is no continuity on the level of political theory, but there is continuity if classical natural right is treated as a doctrine.

There is an ambiguity, or better said, a subtlety in Strauss's analysis that may explain this. At times, Strauss seems to be, in

8   Eric Voegelin, "Israel and Revelation," p. 10.
9   *Nicomachean Ethics*, 1177b33-35, cited by Leo Strauss, *Natural Right and History*, p. 82, n. 1.

some ways, almost "Thomistic" when he expresses appreciation for the Scholastic method of analysis that reached its epitome in St. Thomas's *De Ente et Essentia*.[10] Early in *Natural Right and History* Strauss discerns that our current crisis is defined by our division into "two camps": liberals and Thomists.[11] Strauss's use of the word "doctrine," for example, is inappropriate when it refers to this classic symbolization of Aristotle, but it is appropriate when "doctrine" is used to describe the propositional metaphysics of St. Thomas's natural law theory, or what Strauss refers to as the "Thomistic doctrine of natural right."[12] Surely, not both can be accurately described as a "doctrine." The term "doctrine" has pejorative connotations which Strauss was willing to ignore because, indeed, he was interested in a doctrinal theory of natural right.

Aristotle's ethical inquiry into right by nature is not the same as St. Thomas's propositional metaphysics, and thus a major difference between Voegelin and Straus is Voegelin's preference for Aristotle and his criticism of what he called dogmatism. Voegelin writes in *Anamnesis:*

> Classical noesis...does indeed offer many contact points at which dogmatic misunderstandings could arise, and since these misunderstandings actually arose immediately after Aristotle in the dogmatism of the schools, the *parekbasis* of dogmatism already existed fifteen hundred years before Thomas. But Thomas was the first to crystallize this misunderstanding into "metaphysics" and brought about the perversion of noetic exegesis by terminologically ossifying it into a propositional science of principles, universals and substances.[13]

10 Leo Strauss, *Natural Right and History*, pp. 9, 32.
11 Ibid., p. 7.
12 Ibid., p. 163.
13 Eric Voegelin, *Anamnesis. On the Theory of History and Politics*, M. J. Hanak, trans., *The Collected Works of Eric Voegelin*, Vol. 6 (Columbia: University of Missouri Press, 2002), pp. 391–92.

In a lecture at which I was present, Voegelin went further and argued that St. Thomas's *De ente et essentia* was a final derailment that would lead ultimately to what he called "dogmatomachy." Though Voegelin's rejection of Thomistic propositional reasoning is an interesting topic by itself, it is relevant here because it reveals the key difference between Voegelin and Strauss on "natural right."

Strauss seems to have turned the discussion of why something is right everywhere but is always changing into a form of propositional metaphysics capable of discovering universal rules. Such a doctrinal approach led Strauss to argue that the "unalienable Rights" of the Declaration of Independence stand in a direct line of succession from Aristotle through the natural law doctrine of Scholasticism to the Social Contract thinkers and became the defining intellectual form of the American regime. That mistaken view had a number of consequences. It easily lent itself to what would become a Straussian "school" of propositional metaphysics based on a doctrine of "natural right." As I shall discuss later, when that doctrine was used to define the American regime, it had adverse consequences when that doctrine morphed into a political religion.

Despite Strauss's lack of interest in, or his ignoring of, theology or Biblical revelation, it is significant that Strauss's students report that he re-engaged students who had placed some distance between themselves and the religions of their birth either from estrangement or spiritual dryness.[14] Eric Voegelin's works attracted American students and scholars for whom the Old Testament and the Gospels were more than a distant memory. Most carried the truths of Christianity "in their hips," to use a phrase of Willmoore Kendall, and most students of Voegelin at the University of Notre Dame remembered lessons from attendance at Catholic

---

14   Hadley Arkes, "Strauss on our Minds," in Deutsch, Kenneth L. and Murley, Johan A., eds. *Leo Strauss, the Straussians, and the American Regime* (Rowman & Littlefield Pubs. 1999), p. 86. I am thankful to Dr. Mark Blitz and Dr. Carnes Lord for bringing this collection of essays to my attention.

elementary and secondary schools. The heads of Strauss's and Voegelin's students were filled with ideas, not cannabis or LSD, and they watched with some interest the cultural decline of American churches, the destruction of higher education by a "New Left" in the late 1960s and early 1970s, and the intellectual weakness of elected political leaders who ignorantly expanded the powers and programs of the American administrative state.

As for the conservative "movement," both Voegelin and Strauss were skeptical. Both had experienced "movements" in Europe that were destructive of the order of the West. That may explain Voegelin's criticism of Gerhart Niemeyer for holding an event at the Chicago meeting of the American Political Science Association in 1964 that featured writings by Voegelin that, he complained, could be described as having "a strong slant toward conservative politics."[15] What Leo Strauss may have thought of his student, Harry Jaffa, whose scholarly gifts were used to craft speeches for Barry Goldwater, is an interesting question.

Carnes Lord writes that though Strauss would have welcomed the resurgence of conservatism of the 1970s (Strauss died in 1973), he would not have accepted "the fundamental outlook of the dominant elements in the conservative coalition that emerged in the 1980s,"[16] the era of the "Reagan Revolution."

If that is an accurate assessment, would Voegelin have been similarly disposed? Voegelin's position as a Fellow at the Hoover Institution for more than fifteen years would have put him in close contact with many Hoover scholars who served in the Reagan administration. That familiarity would have shaped his understanding of what was happening in the United States that led to the election of Ronald Reagan. And Voegelin was a realist who understood that Communism represented a dangerous, deformed consciousness, which placed civilization in peril.

15 Thomas Hollweck, ed., *The Collected Works of Eric Voegelin*, Vol. 30, *Selected Correspondence 1950–1984* (University of Missouri Press, 2007), p. 472.
16 Carnes Lord, "Thoughts on Strauss and our Present Discontent," in Deutsch and Morley, *Leo Strauss*, p. 414.

Both Strauss and Voegelin deplored the politicization of scholarship, however. When the author asked Voegelin about the scholarship of Hoover Institution fellows, Voegelin remarked, "Quite good, if your purpose is to work for the next American president."

A sentence in William Galston's essay in *Leo Strauss, the Straussians, and the American Regime* suggests that Voegelin's and Strauss's economic views may also have shaped their views of American politics. Galston, who served as a political appointee in the Clinton administration, writes, "In many respects, after all, the social value of work exceeds its market value."[17] Galston's rejection of unfettered markets is considered heresy by some contemporary American conservatives, but for European political theorists like Voegelin and Strauss, it is likely that "capitalism" would seem ideological and indicative of a closed system that they would have rejected. We should remember also that even Frederick Hayek in the *Constitution of Liberty* was at pains to explore how a free economy can assure "a given minimum of sustenance for all."[18] If given a choice between unfettered free markets and Friedrich Hayek's approach, both Strauss and Voegelin would most likely have chosen Hayek.

Strauss's and Voegelin's experience in Austria and Germany prior to and after World War II would have disposed their students to be critical of "movements." And Voegelin's political theory demanded that the political theorist avoid imposing the dogma of partisan politics on the philosophic quest. Yet, despite their protests, the works of Strauss and Voegelin came to be identified with a conservative "movement." And for many "movement conservatives," Voegelin and Strauss were their theoretical guides.

Unfortunately, Strauss's influence on the American conservative movement does not have a happy ending and this is due to his fascination with the doctrine of "natural right."

17 William Galston, "Cornell Days," ibid., p. 435.
18 F. A. Hayek, *The Constitution of Liberty* (University of Chicago Press, 1960), p. 259.

Like Voegelin, Strauss taught classical Greek philosophy with courses focused on the dialogues of Plato and the works of Aristotle. The students of both Strauss and Voegelin were thus rooted in these classics and their later careers were devoted to teaching these works and, for some, writing analyses of the Greek natural philosophers and the philosophy of Socrates, Plato, and Aristotle. Many prominent scholars in the "Straussian school" contributed to a broader understanding of classical philosophy. However, Strauss's influential *Natural Right and History* revealed a mistaken assumption that the Declaration of Independence rooted the American regime in natural right doctrine.

To a large extent the social disorder of American society today, the general loss of community, the decline of authority, and the disdain that our intellectuals have toward America and all things American, a common acceptance of relativism that is deepening into nihilism, begins in a "natural right" interpretation of the American regime as defined by the Declaration of Independence.[19] Strauss's belief that the American regime via the Declaration of Independence is rooted in natural right doctrine follows from his assumption that "In spite of their opposition to each other, they [Hobbes and classic philosophy] are motivated by fundamentally the same spirit. Their origin is the concern with a right or sound order of society whose actualization is probable. . . ." Treating classical philosophy as equivalent on a moral or theoretical level to modern political theory is troubling. Strauss observes, for example, that Marlowe's statement that Machiavelli held that "there is no sin but ignorance" . . . "is almost a definition of the philosopher" (*Natural Right*, 190–91, 177).

Machiavelli a philosopher?

19   Fr. Stanley Parry, a student of Willmoore Kendall's at Yale and a member of the faculty in the Government Department at Notre Dame, sensed the misdirection of political theory in Strauss's *Natural Right and History* and questioned whether natural right theory is a true theory of man. February 26, 1965 meeting of the Philadelphia Society, Chicago, Illinois. Audio recording may be accessed at www.phillysoc.org at the "Past Meetings" tab.

And the "Discourse on the Origin of Inequality" of Rousseau, Strauss writes, is decidedly the work of a "philosopher" (264). Rousseau, whose writings inspired the Terror of the French Revolution, a philosopher?

And that brings us to this question. If, as Strauss proclaimed, the philosopher is the representative of truth, how can the speculations of Hobbes, Locke, and Rousseau be considered philosophic? In the course of his interpretation of the doctrine of natural right, Strauss works *within* the systems of Hobbes, Locke, and Rousseau, as if they were engaged in inquiries equivalent to the inquiries of the Greek natural philosophers, Socrates, Plato, and Aristotle, and not wholly different. While Strauss certainly sees Hobbes, Locke, and Rousseau in continuity with Plato and Aristotle, his final chapter in *Natural Right and History* takes up the "Crisis" of modern natural right. One could infer from his argument that while the Enlightenment figures are philosophers, their philosophy is problematic. But, Strauss's lack of, or weak, criticism of the "moderns" and his silence in the face of the modern philosophers' rejection of Christianity places Strauss in the ambiguous position of an interpreter of ideas who selectively leaves out those ideas he doesn't want to confront.

Strauss is critical of Max Weber's "fact vs. value dichotomy" and observes that there occurred a "politicization of philosophy in the seventeenth century" (39, 34), but Strauss does not seem to want to acknowledge that Thomas Hobbes, Machiavelli, John Locke, and Jean-Jacques Rousseau engaged in a reversal of classical philosophy that is the hallmark of this "politicization" of philosophy. The modern concepts of these thinkers, the State of Nature, the Law of Nature, the Social Contract and, of course, Natural Rights are not symbols of experience complementary to, or rooted in, the philosophic quest of classical philosophy. They are replacements for that quest, ideological concepts that lead us into a new, modern, era that is, frankly, arrogant and dismissive of philosophic truth.

Hobbes, Locke and Rousseau can be called "modern" in the same sense that Petrarch viewed the conversion of Rome to

Christianity as a "dark age"[20] and revised the Augustinian revaluation of history by asserting that pre-Christian Rome was an age of light and glory.[21] Had Strauss not made the common mistake of treating revelation as "supernatural" (144)[22] he might have been disposed to see the equivalence of experience that engendered classical philosophy and revelation, and, by contrast, that the ideas of Hobbes are not "motivated by fundamentally the same spirit."

While Strauss was pursuing the argument that a doctrine of natural right can be traced from classical philosophy to the modern era, other philosophers were dealing with actual problems of political order. That, I think, distinguishes Strauss from Voegelin and from many of his contemporaries. Strauss's approach in *Natural Right and History* seems irrelevant in the light of the very important analyses of the origins of totalitarianism of Albert Camus in *L'Homme révolté* (1951) and Hannah Arendt's *Origins of Totalitarianism* (1951). They were doing what classical political philosophers do, examining problems in science. Strauss was doing what modern theorists do, developing topics. Although this approach was theoretically deficient, Strauss's analysis of a topic, as opposed to problems of political order, had value for the development of a politically acceptable "School" that had significant consequences as members of that school gained influence in academe and American politics.

This essential difference in the approach between Voegelin and Strauss has generated heated discussions among scholars influenced by them. *Natural Right and History* begins, for example,

---

20 Ephraim Emerton, *The Beginnings of Modern Europe: 1250–1450* (Boston: Ginn and Co., 1917), pp. 464, 480.

21 Erwin Panofsky, *Renaissance and Renascences in Western Art* (New York: Harper and Row, 1972), p. 10.

22 In Book VI of *The City of God*, St. Augustine comments on Varro's *Antiquities* in which Varro divided theology into mythical (fabulous), natural and civil. This led St. Augustine to collapse these three into two, natural and civil, and to add a third, supernatural, category of theology. The unfortunate consequence of this distinction was to relegate revelation to a supernatural, irrational place that reason cannot enter.

with an assertion that the American nation was "conceived and raised" in the propositions of the Declaration of Independence.

For scholars of American political theory influenced by Eric Voegelin such as Willmoore Kendall, Ellis Sandoz, George Carey, Melvin Bradford, Stanley Parry, and historians who are appreciative of the works of David Hackett Fischer, Strauss's statement is a common, but one-sided interpretation of the Declaration of Independence.

What the Declaration actually meant to those Americans infused with the "Spirit of '76" cannot be inferred solely from the Engrossed Copy of the document.[23]

When it came time to articulate why we were engaged in a rebellion against the English Crown, Thomas Jefferson was assigned to write the first draft of what came to be known as a "Declaration of Independence." And, although the first draft of the Declaration of Independence composed by Jefferson was modified by the Committee on Style of the Continental Congress, some Straussian-influenced scholars treat the Engrossed Copy as if it had not gone through an important process of editing from which we can learn much. The Committee on Style, in fact, "caught" most of Jefferson's Enlightenment notions and softened them so as not to offend the dominant Christian culture of colonial America in 1776. Nevertheless, despite that evidence, these interpreters of the Declaration pursue an argument that takes them from Thomas Jefferson to Abraham Lincoln and promotes a redemptive purpose of the American regime.

The Constitution of the United States, not the Declaration, however, is the governing document of the American regime and, before the Constitution was ratified, an unwritten constitution had developed over more than one hundred and eighty years. The American colonies, collectively and independently, contributed to development of a unified consciousness of America's uniqueness and, ultimately, its difference and separateness from

---

23 See my analysis of the three drafts of the Declaration in Richard Bishirjian, *The American Political Tradition*, pp. 52–6.

the mother country. Although that culture was shaped by waves of emigration from England, their principal motivation was religious estrangement from the British establishment. That assured that the experience of Christian religion and faith would be a permanent aspect of the American political order. Ultimately, that spirit led to resistance to both the King and Parliament's claim of the power to rule the colonies without their consent.

One hundred and forty years of colonial history, the experience of freedom, the vastness of the American continent, and the practices of varieties of Christian religion developed into an unwritten constitution and culture of folkways that erupted in a rebellion. That unwritten constitution became "ensouled" in the "Spirit of '76," defined our War of Independence and, ultimately, determined the framing of the Constitution of the Unites States. The imposition of a redemptive mission upon that historical record was a later, ideological, development of humanist intellectuals influenced by European nationalist uprising of the 1840s, liberal Unitarianism, and German Idealism transported to the United States in the form of American Transcendentalism.[24] That "prophetic-utopian" interpretation of the Declaration is, quite simply, based on ideology, not historical evidence.

The heroic efforts of citizen soldiers and the leadership of George Washington and his generals are worthy of any country in world history. Lexington, Concord, Bunker Hill, Quebec, White Plains, Brandywine, Saratoga, Monmouth, Valley Forge, Trenton and, finally, Yorktown, resound with the cries of men willing to sacrifice everything. Few, if any, examples in the histories of this struggle and the earlier colonial era, captured by some of America's finest historians, support a monocausal, Enlightenment, interpretation of the War of Independence.[25]

24 Richard Gamble's important scholarship in his essay, included in a Symposium on American Foreign Policy in *Modern Age* (Fall, 2014), explores this aspect of how an internationalist civil religion had developed long before the American Civil War.

25 In addition to David Hackett Fischer, *Albion's Seed* and his *Washington's Crossing*, my favorites are Fred Anderson, *Crucible of War: The Seven Years'*

THE CONSERVATIVE REBELLION

There was, frankly, much more going on before the first shots were fired at Lexington and Concord than the sound of the turning of pages of Locke's *Second Treatise*. A growing comprehension of the American colonists of their existence "apart from" their relationship with England gradually increased as the American continent grew in territory and wealth, and became self-sufficient. Historian Fred Thompson's study of the French and Indian War also suggests that the American rebellion, like many rebellions, was inspired by pride and resentment at the manner the American "colonials" were treated by what now were seen as "the British." Many "colonials" who fought alongside the British against the French walked away from that experience having decided never again to fight as allies.

Strauss's influence on the development of what some call the "Straussian" school of political theorists is extremely important for the political theory profession in American higher education and in the councils of government. That influence seems to have two sources. One source is Strauss's admirable and influential mastery of classical philosophy. Many of his students have contributed significantly to our understanding of ancient political theory and some recent scholarship on the Progressive movement by Straussian scholars affiliated with the Claremont Review is critical for our understanding of the growth of an all-intrusive administrative state in American political life.[26] However, the other, unfortunate source of Strauss's influence is due to making the "doctrine of natural right" a part of the philosophic discussion of the best regime. Thus, the best regime is committed to the actualization of natural right and natural right is seen as integral to its

---

War and the Fate of Empire in British North America, 1754–1766 and Walter MacDougall, *Promised Land, Crusader State: The American Encounter With the World Since 1776*.

26 John Marini and Kenneth Masugi, *The Progressive Revolution in Politics and Political Science: Transforming the American Regime* (Rowman & Littlefield, 2005). The Claremont Review also maintains an archive of research on the Progressive movement: http://www.claremontinstitute.org/index.php?act=page&id=244&pid=203.

definition. That, of course, is contrary to the original meaning of the classical theory of "right by nature."

Strauss's examination of natural right "doctrine" would have been seen by Voegelin as a philosophic "derailment," a term which Voegelin used to express the eclipse of philosophy grounded in experience. Derailment can take several forms. In the period of transition of Classical philosophy to the speculation of the Stoics, philosophy was deformed into "doctrine." The symbols which Plato and Aristotle created to articulate their experience of reality were evocative of original experience of the sacred. But once philosophy ceases to be a medium of experience, Voegelin writes, "A new intellectual game with imaginary realities in an imaginary realm of thought, the game of propositional metaphysics, has been opened with world historic consequences that reach into our own present."[27] My explanation of this process in *The Development of Political Theory* is still valid:

> The Stoic dogmatization of philosophy, though destructive in its ultimate consequences, had the immediate effect of preserving the insight of Classical philosophy against the inevitable defect that philosophy requires "philosophers" if it is to be preserved. In the absence of persons of the rank of Socrates, Plato, and Aristotle to continue the search for truth, and of circumstances conducive to the contemplative life, the dogmatization of philosophy at least preserved the symbols of philosophy. But the ravages of dogmatism can be contained only so long before they take pernicious forms. For Voegelin, the concept "ideology" represents the final turn in the decline of philosophy when the symbols no longer articulate original experience of theophany, but become the means by which theophany is eradicated from public and personal consciousness.[28]

27   Eric Voegelin, *The Ecumenic Age*, p. 43.
28   Richard Bishirjian, *The Development of Political Theory*, pp. 229–230.

The derailment of Strauss's classical scholarship in his doctrine of natural right has had negative consequences for American foreign policy.

Robert Kagan's important analysis of the development of America in *Dangerous Nation* contains themes that are consistent with Strauss's natural right doctrine. American foreign policy, according to Kagan, was "revolutionary" as a consequence of the struggle for independence from Britain. From that struggle, Kagan writes of the Founders, "They invented a new foreign policy founded upon the universalist ideology that the Revolution spawned." Contrary to the interpretation of the War of Independence by conservatives that the rebellion sought to preserve the rights of Englishmen, Kagan argues that the colonists fought to secure "universal natural rights, granted by God and enjoyed by all men regardless of nationality, culture and history." "The Declaration of Independence was at once an assertion of this radical principle, a justification for rebellion, and the founding document of American nationhood."[29]

In this context, Kagan sees the leaders of the War of Independence as idealists "committed to a set of universal principles." Though statecraft is necessarily focused on the national interest, Kagan argues that the foreign policy of a liberal republic cannot be divorced from principles of liberalism and republicanism. One of the claims of a foreign policy fashioned in this mode is the claim that America never engaged in conquests to gain territory, and our own Civil War was not fought "for interest." It was "a crusade for the good of mankind." All our wars have been selfless quests for "freedom and natural rights" (57, 72, 102, 267, 44).

As with most universal theories, there is some evidence for all of Kagan's claims. Most interesting, for example, is his mention that Thomas Jefferson conferred with the Marquis de Lafayette to draft the French Revolution's Declaration of the Rights of Man (109). But, the story Kagan weaves from the American Founding

---

29 Robert Kagan, *Dangerous Nation*, pp. 40–41. Further citations of this book will be given parenthetically in the text.

to the Civil War too often stretches the historical record in order to make a point. There is, of course, an extreme strain of "moralism" that tends toward self-righteousness that is a part of our heritage as Americans. And, if Kagan had begun *Dangerous Nation* with the events leading up to the American Civil War, he would be making a better argument.

From Abraham Lincoln to Woodrow Wilson, a new strain of political religion enters American history, gains strength, and shapes twentieth and twenty-first-century American history. And, although Woodrow Wilson's political religion has become the most powerful force in American political life, Abraham Lincoln also contributed to the acculturation of American citizens to political religion by utilizing Biblical language in his construction of the meaning of democracy.

Some of Lincoln's religious language comes, Kagan suggests, from the Second Great Awakening. Lincoln, too, rejected self-interest as the sole guide in foreign policy. In that respect, Kagan's claim that a "universalist ideology" alone shaped our polity is overwhelmed by other evidence he provides that a pervasive moral sense is evident throughout our history. Universalist ideology and moral sensitivity are not the same. Kagan duly cites evidence of the rise of a uniquely American "moralism." The first annual address of John Quincy Adams, for example, states that government is instituted for "the progressive improvement of the condition of the governed." American "moralism" was also evident in public reaction to the war between Christian Greeks and the "Muslim Turks." A similar public response occurred when Louis Kossuth, leader of the uprising of Hungarians against the Hapsburgs in 1848, sought the support of the American people. And Kagan notes that Abraham Lincoln offered a resolution supporting the universal right of self-determination at a Kossuth meeting in 1852. The Second Great Awakening, Kagan writes, aroused moral outrage in the North against the South. And in the war against Spain, the motivating force was not our universalist liberal ideology, but our compassion for the horrible suffering of Cuban citizens forced into "reconcentration" camps (261, 151, 169, 255, 256, 194, 391).

Americans are easily motivated to redress a moral wrong and not solely by the complex of ideas that make up the American political religion.

That political religion, fully developed in Wilsonian idealism,[30] overwhelms attention to the moralistic motives of our intervention in World War I, the "Crusade" which described the our engagement in World War II, the military defense of the "right to self-determination" of the South Vietnamese that Lyndon Johnson used to justify the war in Vietnam, the Balkan intervention by the Clinton administration, the invasions of Afghanistan and Iraq of the George W. Bush administration. Even today, calls for interventions around the world to protect women are made from feminist ideology and moralistic reasoning.

With the fall of the Soviet Union, the coalition of forces within the Republican Party lost an anchor that tethered them to a common foreign policy. Anti-communism was the glue that held together Libertarians, Evangelical and millenarian Christians, "country club" Republicans, the remaining members of the Eisenhower and Rockefeller wings of the Republican Party, supply-side economists, Reagan Democrats, traditional political conservatives, and anti-communist liberals who came to be called "Neoconservatives." Absent that threat to our national survival, the Republican-Conservative coalition could not hold, nor could it act effectively. After the collapse of the Soviet Union, George H. W. Bush was unable to design a unifying vision for his administration. When faced with a recession, President Bush broke his word, raised taxes, and cut the only ties he had to economic conservatives. In the presidential contest of 1992, forty-seven years after the end of World War I, the electoral power of the "Greatest Generation" had weakened with age and a younger candidate, William Jefferson Clinton, defeated the last President who had fought in the Second World War.

A political vacuum existed that was filled by a neoconservative

30 See my analysis of Wilsonian idealism in Richard Bishirjian, "Wilson, Croly and the American Civil Religion," *Modern Age* 23 (Winter, 1979), 33–38.

"Statement of Principles" issued by the Project for the New American Century in June, 1997, and signed by twenty-five Republican leaders.[31] "Project" staff and directors included William Kristol and Robert Kagan.

Though admirable in its patriotic sentiments and its call for revival of "a Reaganite policy of military strength and moral clarity," in hindsight, the Statement of Principles was used to advocate, and slavishly justify, the imperial policies of President George W. Bush. In the wake of that administration's imperial policies, the nation's financial resources were exhausted, the lives of yet another generation of young Americans were sacrificed in wars committed to nation-building, new and costly welfare programs were instituted that expanded the administrative state in a Department of Homeland Security. Neoconservative influence destroyed the hard-won, limited-government, "brand" of the Republican Party.

In 1997, though not today, we might have missed the ideological "tone" of the Project for the New American Century to "shape a new century," to maintain a strong military that can meet "future challenges," the need to meet our "responsibilities of global leadership," and pursue a role "in maintaining peace and security in Europe, Asia, and the Middle East," and the need "to shape circumstances before crises emerge." The "Statement" ends with a call to embrace a "cause."

Anyone familiar with nineteenth-century ideologies and the manifestos with which they announced their arrival in the world can sense the ideological character of the Project for the New

---

31 Signers of the "Statement of Principles" are Elliott Abrams. Gary Bauer, William J. Bennett, John Ellis "Jeb" Bush, Dick Cheney, Eliot A. Cohen, Midge Decter, Paula Dobriansky, Steve Forbes, Aaron Friedberg, Francis Fukuyama, Frank Gaffney, Fred C. Ikle, Donald Kagan, Zalmay Khalilzad, I. Lewis "Scooter" Libby, Norman Podhoretz, J. Danforth Quayle, Peter W. Rodman, Stephen P. Rosen, Henry S. Rowen, Donald Rumsfeld, Vin Weber, George Weigel, Paul Wolfowitz. Though the Project for the New American Century has disbanded, its basic documents are archived on the Web: http://web.archive.org/web/20070810113753/http://www.newamerican-century.org/statementofprinciples.htm.

American Century. Theirs is not a call to determine carefully the
American national interest, anticipate and prepare to respond to
challenges to that national interest, and assess our ability to engage in future wars. Manifestos are not grounded in philosophic
reason, but in propositional reasoning motivated by a "cause."[32]
The pathology of a "cause" was evident in President George W.
Bush's call, in his Second Inaugural, for the "expansion of freedom in all the world."

> The survival of liberty in our land increasingly depends
> on the success of liberty in other lands. The best hope
> for peace in our world is the expansion of freedom in
> all the world.
>
> America's vital interests and our deepest beliefs are
> now one. From the day of our Founding, we have pro-
> claimed that every man and woman on this earth has
> rights, and dignity, and matchless value, because they
> bear the image of the Maker of Heaven and earth.
> Across the generations we have proclaimed the imper-
> ative of self-government, because no one is fit to be a
> master, and no one deserves to be a slave. Advancing
> these ideals is the mission that created our Nation. It is
> the honorable achievement of our fathers. Now it is the
> urgent requirement of our nation's security, and the
> calling of our time.
>
> So it is the policy of the United States to seek and
> support the growth of democratic movements and in-
> stitutions in every nation and culture, with the ultimate
> goal of ending tyranny in our world.

These "insights," shared with the American people at George W.
Bush's second inauguration, are derived from the Declaration of
Independence.

---

32 I examine the "cause" of a New World Order in Richard Bishirjian, "Origins
    and End of the New World Order," *Modern Age* 46 (Summer 2004), 200.

When the Declaration of Independence was first read in public and the Liberty Bell was sounded in celebration, a witness said, "It rang as if it meant something." In our time, it means something still. America, in this young century, proclaims liberty throughout all the world and to all the inhabitants thereof. Renewed in our strength, tested but not weary, we are ready for the greatest achievements in the history of freedom.

Today, as a consequence of this uniquely American political religion, the American nation is financially at risk, overextended by commitments to the self-determination of other countries, and so weakened intellectually and militarily that challenges to our national interest from Iran, China, and Russia lack a convincing response.

Is there a solution?

Only if American statecraft can return to its roots in the national interest, if politicians replace the political religion of "democracy" with serious consideration of our national interest, and we educate our statesmen to be representatives of America and not global citizens.

Chapter 8
Recovery

Almost fifty years ago, Fr. Stanley Parry was a principal speaker at the first meeting of members of a new conservative organization. The Philadelphia Society was formed after the presidential election of 1964 by conservative activist Donald Lipsett. Lipsett had been Midwest Director of the Intercollegiate Studies Institute who, for many years, had organized seminars and presentations by major conservative academics for college students in the Midwest. The first organizational and membership meetings of the Philadelphia Society in 1964 and 1965 were gatherings of conservative luminaries of the twentieth century: University of Chicago economist Milton Friedman, University of Michigan historian Stephen Tonsor, Stanford University scholars Stephen Possony and Robert Strausz-Hupé, Hoover Institution director W. Glenn Campbell, Romance Language scholar and philosopher Thomas Molnar, former Yale University political scientist Willmoore Kendall, National Review contributing editor Frank Meyer, independent scholar Russell Kirk, Gerhart Niemeyer, and many more.

Fr. Stanley Parry's presentation at the 1965 membership meeting of the Philadelphia Society has been preserved and may be accessed at the website of the Society.[1] Is there a Plato or Augustine to guide us, he asked? There is certainly a need for someone to ask the Socratic questions that challenge our basic assumptions. But, that philosophy is yet to be born, and when it is born it will not be a "conservative

---

1   Stanley Parry, C.S.C, "The Real Problem of the Conservative Theory," Philadelphia Society, Chicago, February 26, 1965. Available online: http://phillysoc.org/tps_meetings/the-future-of-freedom-the-problems-and-the-prospects

philosophy" because philosophy is universal and will ask questions that are very upsetting to a society that is upside down.

Fr. Parry's presentation is relevant for our understanding of the Conservative Rebellion since what began as a rebellion against ideologies of the Left has become entangled in a competition for leadership of the conservative movement. The Rebellion begun in twentieth-century America stood united against Soviet communism and Progressive era Liberalism and now, in the twenty-first century, the destruction of that unity is apparent.

This analysis of the Conservative Rebellion argues that a principal cause of this condition of disunity is a civil religion of natural right that morphed into a dangerous, redemptive, immanentist, political religion that committed the United States to redeem the world for democracy. The first eruption of this political religion by official act of an American president occurred during the administration of President Woodrow Wilson. Wilson's political religion was shaped by more than half a century of redemptionist speculation by Unitarian religious leaders and American Transcendentalists who responded to the national movements that disrupted Europe beginning in the 1840s.[2] This civil religion's first official appearance in the formulation of President Abraham Lincoln's Gettysburg Address and Second Inaugural have provided an intellectual substructure shaping how later generations of Americans interpret the American nation's essential being. Lincoln's civil religion, though pregnant with revolutionary possibilities, is not the same as the full-blown political religion of Presidents Woodrow Wilson or George W. Bush.

Civil religion is the articulation of national purpose in religious symbols. Political religion is an ideology that rejects reality and seeks to replace it with a this-worldly salvation. That has been a permanent disruptive force in American political life since the presidency of Woodrow Wilson and threatens the stability and order of normal life whenever it erupts.

---

2   Richard Gamble, "The Battle Hymn of the Republic," *Modern Age* (Fall 2014).

At the end of the Ice Age, when glaciers began to recede, large and small pieces of the larger mass broke off and formed what we call "detritus." Detritus from the recession of conservative unity in the twentieth century is what is left today of a Conservative Rebellion that gave unity to the response of the United States to the disruptions, revolutions and wars of that era.

Several claimants now contend for leadership of the Conservative Rebellion and offer to lead us Rebels out of the abyss into which the American nation has fallen. Their seductive appeals tend to be limited, however. None has an all-encompassing philosophy of order.

There are five claimants whose appeals have been influential.

Neoconservatives believe in a political religion of democracy and appeal to use of America's military force in service to the advance of democracy throughout the world.

Laissez-faire capitalism appeals to economics and economic growth, but excludes, or has nothing to say about, the spiritual aspects of man.

Radical Traditionalism is a more recent contender for leadership, with particular appeal to intellectuals. Radical Traditionalists criticize Enlightenment notions that were current at the founding of the Constitution of the United States and point to the possibility of a better regime, unaffected by, or cleansed of, bad philosophy.

Millenarian Christians appeal to the Biblical promise of a Second Coming which they hope to advance by applying Scripture to foreign policy.

And, lastly, there are the Tea Party conservatives.

I. Neoconservatives

The defeat of President George H. W. Bush by William Jefferson Clinton in 1992 gave Progressives yet another opportunity to grow the administrative state—their fourth such opportunity in ninety-six years.[3] President Bush's defeat was significant also be-

---

3   Republicans, of course, are not immune, but except for Richard Nixon and George W. Bush, few exceeded the growth in state powers under Presidents Wilson, Roosevelt, Truman, Kennedy, Johnson, Carter, Clinton and Obama.

cause he was the last American president to have fought in World War II.

A new era had begun and we Conservative Rebels were destined to see both victory and defeat. What might have become a conservative rout was pushed back in 1994 by Newt Gingrich's "Contract with America." Instead of the platitudes from an earlier era of World War II Republicans, a younger generation, led by a quirky professor of history, appealed to the American people for a reversal of the policies of the previous half-century. Republicans took control of the U.S. House of Representatives for the first time since 1952. Thus, the election of George W. Bush in the 2000 election was welcomed by Conservative Texans who knew "W" from his days as Governor of Texas and who were close observers of his father's presidency. The spending binge of Republicans during the administration of George W. Bush was bad enough, but his invasion of Iraq and commitment to "nation-building" in Afghanistan after the Taliban regime was removed, had permanent consequences. Not only were American troops subjected to long-term commitments of occupation of Muslim countries, the removal of Saddam Hussein from the balance of power between Iran and Iraq increased the influence in Southwest Asia of an Iranian theocracy determined to become a nuclear power. The imperial policies of President George W. Bush's administration's reflected a response to the successful terrorist attack on the World Trade Center on September 11, 2001 and the rise of Islam. Those events coincided with the growing influence of Neoconservatives.

In the 1970s, Democrats, unhappy with the successful takeover of the Democratic Party by McGovern Democrats, began to align themselves with the Republican Party. During the 1930s these aspiring intellectuals aligned with the Trotskyite wing of the communist movement, and by the 1960s, firmly situated in the Democratic Party, they had no difficulty enthusiastically endorsing the big government policies of Lyndon Johnson. They believed that the American people want big government. But when the Hubert Humphrey and Scoop Jackson wing of the Democratic Party was overrun by Leftist forces, anti-communist Liberals like

Irving Kristol, Midge Decter, Norman Podhoretz, Jeanne Kirk-patrick and others nominally on the Left, moved swiftly to the Right. Though small in numbers, they were enormously influential through publications like Commentary, The Public Interest and The National Interest, and, later, a second generation of Neoconservatives launched The Weekly Standard. Now recognized as "Neoconservatives" and fueled by grants from foundations[4] under their control, they completed their march to national power by taking control of the American Enterprise Institute and infiltrating their numbers into the presidential administrations of Ronald Reagan and George H. W. Bush. In distinguishing between first and second generation Neoconservatives, it bears repeating the words of the "Godfather" of Neoconservatism, Irving Kristol, since William Kristol is a main advocate of a new generation of Neoconservatism.

> . . . once upon a time, in this country the question of democracy was a matter for political philosophy rather than for faith. And the way in which a democratic political philosophy was gradually and inexorably transformed into a democratic faith seems to me to be perhaps the most important problem in American intellectual, and ultimately political history.[5]

Fatefully, in the late 1990s, a second generation of Neoconservatives leaders, William Kristol and Ronald Kagan, embraced the "democratic faith" that the Godfather gave reason to abjure, called for a redemptive American foreign policy from a new entity—the Project for the New American Century. Their ability to raise money from corporate America was formidable and their commitment and financial support of ideas and the intellectual class associated

4   The Bradley, Olin and Randolph Foundations were administered by persons recommended by Irving Kristol. Kristol used his influence to assure that a Neoconservative, William Bennett, would become Chairman of the National Endowment of the Humanities.
5   Irving Kristol, *On the Democratic Idea in America*, p. 51.

with the Neoconservative movement gave them a megaphone that was far louder than their actual numbers. Wars sell newspapers, thus it is significant that Rupert Murdoch's News Corp financed the Neoconservative Weekly Standard. A consistent advocate for intervention in Iraq and Afghanistan and calling for invasion of Iran, the Weekly Standard well served the material interests of News Corp. And when the tide of public opinion turned against war lust, Rupert Murdoch sold the Weekly Standard to Philip Anschutz, a Colorado entrepreneur with an interest in religion. Anschutz is the owner of Regal Cinema, and has invested in feature films ("The Chronicles of Narnia" and "Holes") and media venues including the San Francisco Examiner and the Washington Examiner, in addition to the Weekly Standard.

Though limited in numbers and influence within the Republican Party during Reagan's first term, by the end of Reagan's second term, Neoconservatives were firmly entrenched in political appointments at the highest levels of government. A successful terrorist attack on the World Trade Center on September 11, 2001 further enhanced Neoconservative influence. By 2004, Neoconservatives held positions of influence in the White House, the Defense Department and the U.S. Department of State.

The eclipse of traditional conservatives in the area of foreign policy and international relations in the Reagan and subsequent Republican presidential administrations began with the resignation of Richard V. Allen as National Security Advisor to President Reagan. That removed a firm, conservative, influence on Reagan administration foreign policy. And those conservatives given political appointments in the Reagan administration, many with Richard Allen's help, did not survive into Reagan's second term. Thus the Reagan administration 's foreign policy and national security appointments feature Nixon administration moderates and failed to grow the presence of movement conservatives as political appointees in foreign policy posts.[6] And President Reagan, like

6   See my analysis of this in "The Reagan Flaw," The Review of Politics, Vol. 49, Summer 1987, No. 3, pp. 435–37.

most American politicians, knew little to nothing about foreign affairs. That was not the case with Neoconservatives who were advanced in the Reagan administration and the successor administration of George Herbert Walker Bush. That assured that the foreign policy appointments of George W. Bush would take on a Neoconservative "look." To that was added a uniquely millennialist feature provided by an influential speechwriter, Michael J. Gerson.[7]

The use of military force during the administration of George W. Bush was reinforced by Neoconservative enthusiasm for advancing "democracy." Too little attention was given to the national interest and a curious condominium of secular Neoconservatives and Millenarian Christians was fashioned. So-called "Paleoconservatives" took umbrage and a split in the conservative movement occurred that has led to angry accusations, deterioration of personal friendships, and bitter feelings only slightly assuaged by the loss of influence of Neoconservative ideas in the wake of the destruction of the Republican "brand" by President George W. Bush.

The terrorist attack on September 11, 2001, certainly impelled the administration of George W. Bush to engage in policies aimed at Islamic terrorists. Those policies had long-term negative consequences, however. The Patriot Act, and Presidential Executive Orders issued in a War on Terror clearly engaged in overreach and fostered a domestic intelligence system that violated constitutionally protected rights. Calling back these powers from the NSA, CIA, Department of Homeland Security and FBI will be difficult and, while that is attempted, a web of intelligence is primed for use by any President of the United States who desires to inflict injury on his political enemies. These excesses effectively destroyed the Republican "brand" and created the conditions that led to the election of a radical President of the United States

7   Michael J. Gerson, *Heroic Conservatism: Why Republicans Need to Embrace America's Ideals (And Why They Deserve to Fail If They Don't)* (New York: HarperCollins, 2007).

sometimes described as one part Saul Alinsky, one part left-liberal academic, and one part black liberationist.

II. Radical Traditionalists

Radical Traditionalists are new to the Rebellion, but are beginning to grow in influence. Originating in England as "Radical Orthodoxy" by John Milbank and Catherine Pickstock, some orthodox theologians began to reject liberal Christianity and the gods of bourgeois capitalism. In an interview in 2001, Pickstock explained that Radical Orthodoxy entailed a commitment to socialist politics.

> So by "socialism" I mean something like opposition to economic exchange organized only for the maximization of production and profit. An envisaged socialist alternative would not be in terms of State control but of the reorganization of production and exchange *on a cooperative basis*, which might take many different forms. For me, socialism is only possible on the basis of some shared vision of the good.[8]

Similarly, Milbank in 2008 explained in an interview:

> To my mind then, modernity is liberalism, liberalism is capitalism ("political economy") and capitalism is atheism and nihilism.
>
> We're now at a crossroads. Politics is shadow play. In reality economic and cultural liberalism go together and increase together. The left has won the cultural war and the right the economic one. But of course they are really both on the same side.
>
> The point is to resist this. And that means of course, re-think Christendom. But now in more festive,

8 Interview by Strattford Caldecott, published in Second Spring, **http://www.secondspring.co.uk/articles/scaldecott24.htm**

pro-body, yet more interpersonal, less fearing terms and ones celebrating much more excellence and virtue in every realm including those of craft, farming and trade. And having a greater will to the democratization of excellence.[9]

In the United States the Radical Orthodoxy movement is practiced by some conservative political theorists, distributist economists and orthodox theologians and is, thus, more political and economic. Commonly referred to as "Radical Traditionalism," its representatives include University of Notre Dame political scientist Patrick Deneen, Catholic apologist John Rao, and "Distributist" theologian John C. Médaille among others. At the 2011 organizational meeting of the Ciceronian Society, Patrick Deneen's paper titled "The Conservative Case Against the Constitution" criticized the Enlightenment aspects of the thought of James Madison and Alexander Hamilton. Deneen's close reading of Madison's and Hamilton's contributions to the Federalist Papers show that the Constitution of Madison and Hamilton

> establishes a modern republic, shaped in the wake of the philosophy of Machiavelli, Hobbes and Locke, and informed by the goal of human liberation that requires the accumulation of power toward the end of liberating humanity from the constraints of nature. There should be little surprise that this basic ambition ends up conserving very little.

Radical Traditionalists like Deneen highlight Enlightenment influences on the framers of the Constitution and ignore or discount the long history of an "unwritten constitution" that developed

9   Three Questions on Modern Atheism: An Interview with John Milbank Interview by Ben Suriano, TheOtherJournal.com, http://theotherjournal.com/2008/06/04/three-questions-on-modern-atheism-an-interview-with-john-milbank.

during one hundred and eighty years of colonial American history. This is not the place to cite chapter and verse, or more specifically Madison's Notes of the Federal Convention, that reveal a much deeper appreciation of philosophy than is found in the Federalist. But, let us be mindful that though the "mechanistic" language of checks and balances institutionalized in the Constitution of the United States may be insufficient grounds for limiting man's lust for power, they are the only institutional bulwark we have against threats to our freedoms by the American administrative state. Radical Traditionalists forget, however, that the foundations of our political order are fragile and that the Founders are deserving of our respect, not our criticism.

Deneen and other "RadTrads" trained in Departments of Political Science have an obligation to be rigorous in thought, but that also requires a close look at what alternatives there may be to the existing order. In his Ciceronian Society presentation, Deneen points to a possible dialogue with "environmentalists," the reasoning of pacifist Wendell Berry and our need to conserve our reserves of water and oil. In other words, move to the Left.

Deneen's other writings are also informative, such as an essay in The American Conservative magazine for March 25, 2014 titled "Even If Hobby Lobby Wins, We Lose." Here, too, Deneen engages in a thorough critique of modern capitalism. Deneen writes of American commerce:

> Its stores are located generally in the middle of nowhere, in a sea of asphalt, providing the simulacra of ancient craft with goods produced by Chinese and transported by massive container ships, accessible only by automobiles generally by people living in suburbs. They have contributed to the displacing of smaller, local businesses with the extensive assistance of government, especially in the form of free-trade agreements, military-protected fossil-fuel production and transportation along with international shipping corridors, state-sponsored infrastructure that give major advantages to

businesses that rely heavily on economies of scale based on trucking, and zoning laws that encourage the evisceration of downtowns in favor of national chains. Purchases in these chain stores result in a net outflow of money from these communities into the coffers of distant and absentee owners.

Because Deneen's critique of capitalism went beyond "capitalism" to a critique of American commerce as capitalistic, I felt it was necessary to write to the editor of *The American Conservative* with this criticism of Deneen's essay:

> Deneen has clearly engaged in a reconsideration of what freedom is, should and should not be, and his critique of market economics is part and parcel with his critique of Constitutional government (in a paper given at a Ciceronian Society event). Deneen doesn't like the Constitution and free markets because of their origins in Enlightenment reasoning.
>
> Deneen has rejected free markets with a spirit or aspiration for something else. It would be interesting to know more about what that "other" better and brave new world is besides aesthetically appealing architecture that conceals the diseased transactions of a market economy. Perhaps he's thinking of the placid university campuses that he inhabits like Georgetown and Notre Dame where former Catholics overbuild in order to lure fools to send their children to be reeducated—at great cost?
>
> Surely these great "non-profit" commercial enterprises are worthy of an equal critique, though that gets a bit close to Deneen's own sources of income. As to what Deneen's brave new world is, should it permit religious or ethical institutions to tax economic transactions? How about prohibition of alcohol? In Deneen's brave new world are state lotteries preferable to those run by the Mafia?

Perhaps he would have us recreate "Guilds" that act to block those container ships crammed with trinkets from Asia. Deneen, himself, could become the head of a "Guild of Intellectuals."

Should zoning regulations take aim at the spiritually desolate landscapes where corporations market products to individuals now consumed by appeals to shop?

Whatever form this brave new world takes, it must of necessity involve very unconservative coercion, the intrusion of some higher authority—whether of the administrative state or voluntary associations (like accreditation agencies)—to purify, constrain and ultimately control the actions of markets.

But what are markets and what are their origins?

Drill down and you'll find an entrepreneur who, in Deneen's world, is probably a form of vermin or virus whose creative energies eat at the soft tissue of civil society. This, definitely, should be stopped. On that score, Deneen should be pleased that the actions of the Obama Administration are doing precisely that.

Political theorists at Catholic and Protestant colleges attracted to Radical Traditionalism should heed Gerhart Niemeyer's warning: "The critic who forgets that he is a citizen produces not a changed order but sheer disorder."[10] Though some Radical Traditionalists bring a refreshing openness to "religion" and the use of theology in the exploration of social issues and topics, it is less clear that they are engaged in reflection on experience of participation in divine reality as opposed to the ideological rejection of material reality in light of an imagined, more perfect, heavenly world revealed by criticism of the Founders. That, I suggest, explains the undertone of possible use of coercion for a good cause, or in battle with debased reason, that I sense in the writings of some "Rad-Trads."

10   Gerhart Niemeyer, *Between Nothingness and Paradise*, p. 206.

III. Laissez-faire capitalism

"RadTrad" criticism of capitalism and the emphasis on material man in modern American life has its mirror opposite among economists and libertarians for whom economic man, material interests, and autonomous freedoms are valued over any metaphysical interest in the public interest or the common good.

This passage from a presentation by economist Norman Ture[11] in 1995 at St. Vincent College is representative:

> I cannot aspire to delineate the common good, let alone what the common good dictates for a tax system. I am reluctant to assume the role of social philosopher. In the ideological and analytical context of my work, the expression "the common good" when used in connection with any field of public policy implies some notion of a societal utility function. On analytical grounds, the notion is untenable; the view of society as an organic entity with preferences and antipathies distinct from the those of the individuals who comprise it defies delineation in rigorous theoretical terms. On ideological grounds, the notion is reprehensible to people who prize individual freedom and responsibility; it is the essential underpinning of authoritarian societies. In a free society, public policy cannot and must not seek to define and pursue the common good.[12]

Austrian economists Ludwig von Mises and Friedrich Hayek, monetarist Milton Friedman, not to mention Adam Smith, are lodestones of an individualistic focus of politics and economics

11 See this memorial to Norman Ture published by the Institute for Research on the Economics of Taxation at http://www.iret.org/memorial.html.
12 Institute for Research on the Economics of Taxation, http://iret.org/pub_ture/Taxes%20and%20the%20Good%20 Society%201995-Sep.pdf .

of an important sector of the American conservative community. Commonly lumped into one kettle and called "laissez-faire economics," there is a subtle difference between economists like Hayek and those who, like Friedman, advocate a radical individualist ethic. Milton Friedman's advocacy of expanding our freedom to choose does not carry with it an admonition to choose what is right. Likewise, supply-side economists, perhaps the best and certainly most practical of all economic theorists in America today, are not primarily concerned about deficits and expansion of the administrative state so long as deficits are proportional to Gross Domestic Product. The Conservative Rebellion against the secular administrative state isn't the first concern of pro-growth economists.

Criticism of "root canal" Republicans and, particularly, Kansas Senator Bob Dole derided by Cong. Newt Gingrich as a "tax collector for the welfare state," are good fun, but this humor does not expose the proven willingness of the American public to vote *for* spending programs and to vote *against* those who raised taxes to reduce deficits. Of course, too often those who raised taxes saying they would reduce deficits somehow forgot the last part of the bargain. Reducing government expenditures as a percentage of GDP, however, doesn't address the greater issue that the American administrative state is a primary threat to American freedom.

It is evident that, since World War I, a great transformation of public sentiment and character has occurred that makes it difficult to caution restraint. The tax reductions of Harding and Coolidge led to an exuberant era called "The Roaring Twenties." And though a part of that roaring sound was the sound of economic growth made possible by lower taxes and cuts in government spending, another part of that sound was the result of loosening of restraints on the animal appetites of a generation bursting out of the constraints imposed by World War I, Prohibition, and increased discretionary income. Clearly, man does not live by bread alone, but that something else that nourishes his spirit is elusive in twentieth-century America.

IV. Millenarian Christians

Christian Millenarians[13] and religious millennnialists who seek to establish heaven on earth—at least for a time—are also on the American scene with a powerful religious message of redemption that breaches the barrier between the City of Man and the City of God constructed in fifth century by St. Augustine.

In the book of Revelation, Chapter 19, John sees heaven open and a white horse ridden by one who is called Faithful and True. The armies in heaven follow him, and the nations of the earth are destroyed. The Devil is sealed in hell for a thousand years, during which time the righteous reign with Christ. At the end of this millennium, the dead are resurrected and there occurs a Last Judgment. St. Augustine interpreted that prophecy metaphorically and rebukes Millenarians who maintained that the thousand years of the prophecy must be interpreted as meaning a worldly enjoyment of luxury on earth enduring for a thousand years.

"Fundamentalist" Christians who take a literalist approach to the prophecy of a millennium in the Book of Revelation confuse Biblical accounts of ancient Israel with the state of modern Israel. Principled Christians must recognize that we are a nation of laws and men and the policies of Christian politicians should be informed by the law, not Biblical prophecies. If that is ignored, they open themselves to appeals to support policies that may conflict with American national interests.

George W. Bush, unlike his father, George H. W. Bush, experienced a religious conversion that enabled him to overcome addictions that threatened to destroy his life. Though belief in a literal interpretation of the millennium by President Bush cannot be confirmed, a mixture of Wilsonian idealism and immanentist religious eschatology in the foreign policy of the administration of George W. Bush may be attributed to the influence on President Bush of an obscure graduate of Wheaton University.

Michael J. Gerson had been working as a journalist at US

---

13 See Clifford A. Kiracofe, *Dark Crusade. Christian Zionism and US Foreign Policy* (London: I.B. Taurus & Co., 2009).

News and World Report when called to Austin, Texas for an interview with Texas Governor George W. Bush. Gerson relates that Bush told him that he had read his writings and wanted him to start as speechwriter for Bush's campaign for President. Bush had obviously spotted a similarity in Gerson to his own experience of having been "born again" and Gerson became an important influence on the policies of the Bush administration. Though Gerson disavows that he or President Bush affirm a belief in millenarianism,[14] Gerson's history of that administration, titled *Heroic Conservatism*, is replete with statements justifying the use of American might to redeem the world.

> Taking the Declaration of Independence seriously introduces into conservatism a radical belief in the rights of every individual, and a conviction that government must act, when appropriate, to secure those rights when they are assaulted by oppression, poverty and disease.[15]

> Our goal is to move regimes toward political pluralism, without destructive destabilization. This is not a reckless undertaking; it is an unavoidable one. It calls for steady purpose, not mood swings of elation and despair. But there must be a sense of urgency. The question is not: are we pushing for reform too early? A different question hangs over America and the world: are we pushing for reform too late?[16]

> Those who bet on the durability of the current order in the Middle East are not "realists"; they are in denial. And the only serious alternatives to that order are, on the one hand, the disciplined and ruthless forces of rad-

14 Michael J. Gerson, *Heroic Conservatism*, p. 99.
15 Ibid., p 270.
16 Ibid., p. 240.
17 Ibid., p. 239.

ical Islam and, on the other hand, the scattered forces of democracy and reform.[17]

Gerson rejects the assertion that his identification of himself and his President with the will of God is "messianic arrogance."[18] Whether Gerson's musings reflect a traditional belief in Providence or a Gnostic heresy is a question that is important because Gerson fashioned the words spoken by an American president whose policies destroyed the Republican Party. The failure of the George W. Bush administration and the destruction of the Republican brand that was the result of these policies seriously damaged the ability of all Christians to speak to modern America.

The presence of persons of religious faith in American life, however, is critical in the contest between Fourth Paradigm immanentist eschatology and the Fifth Paradigm Conservative Rebellion. For that reason we must lament that Evangelical religious institutions that adhere to a "Biblical worldview," the inerrancy of Scripture, Creationism, and the divinity of Christ are perceived as beyond the pale of modern American culture.

The rejection of Evangelical Christians is one of a piece with the rejection of traditional conservatives from positions in academe, major media, grant-giving foundations and public service. Liberal democratic culture fosters a relativistic ethic that rejects the affirmation of truths while affirming a posture of "openness" that is a disguise for anti-religious and political bias. Thus, though many Evangelical churches support institutions of higher learning, they find that their attempts to import Biblical-based scholarship into secular American culture is simply a century and a half behind where American culture is today.

We must ask, therefore, is there a place for Christian colleges and universities, or even "conservative" institutions of higher learning, in the system of American higher education?

James Piereson argues in The Weekly Standard that, "The left university should not be replaced by the right university. It

18   Ibid., p. 79.

should be replaced by the real university, dedicated to liberal education and higher learning."[19]

Though Piereson's analysis describes how the liberal university was transformed during the civil disturbances of the 1960s and 1970s into a "Left University," and sheds light on the current crisis in higher education, his preference for an ideal of "the real university" is reminiscent of the memoirs of French aristocrats lamenting the French Revolution.

Piereson simply ignores a fundamental reality that you cannot replace something with nothing.

The only cultural forces in twenty-first-century America that are positioned to recapture the ideal of liberal learning are the few remaining Christian colleges that have not betrayed Christ and a small number of politically conservative colleges and universities.

Piereson disdains them in a wistful appeal to academic objectivity.

In other words, for Piereson, the Conservative Rebellion has no role to play in higher education. Such a posture is curious in that Piereson is a Senior Fellow and Director of the Manhattan Institute's Center for the American University and contributing editor of "Minding the Campus." That Internet-based publication is dedicated to "Reforming Our Universities." If Conservative Rebels and Evangelical Christians are rejected as instruments for university reform, where may the political and intellectual resources for recovery be found?

V. Tea Party Conservatives

At this point when all has appeared lost, a new political phenomenon appeared yelling "Stop!"

Just where exactly those affiliated with the Tea Party have been since the Conservative Rebellion began has yet to be determined. Older conservatives who responded to Barry Goldwater,

---

19 James Piereson, "The Left University," The Weekly Standard, October 3, 2005, Vol. 11, No. 3.

and fought alongside Ronald Reagan as he sought the Republican presidential nomination three times, are dumbfounded by the sudden appearance of Tea Party activists. Where were they when we Conservative Rebels went down to defeat in 1964, 1976, 1992 and 1996? And where were they when it became apparent that George H. W. Bush and George W. Bush were big government Republicans committed to an internationalist New World Order?

Clearly, they were not thinking about politics and were assuming that civil society was on autopilot. When the banking crisis of 2008 revealed how quickly an economy could be destroyed and political order disrupted by the election of a radical President, only then did they turn out to protest policies that have been the focus of the Conservative Rebellion since 1964.

To some extent, Tea Party conservatives, sometimes called the "silent majority," have always been present in American politics as exemplified by the many contrarians affiliated with third party Libertarians and, more recently, with the populist anti-government movement of Cong. Ron Paul. With a clear target visible in the socialist policies of Barack Obama, Tea Party contrarians aspire to have considerable influence on future American politics.

VI. Daimonic Men and "Recovery"

Most readers of The Conservative Rebellion share a sense that we live in an era of civilizational decline. Thus we must be aware of the greater context of the collapse of a common civilization that was assured by America's entry into World War I. That willful, fantastical and unnecessary action by an American president who aimed to destroy the system of European balance-of-power politics opened a Pandora's box from which sprang Lenin, Stalin, Hitler and Mussolini. The destruction of order of these modern totalitarians released intellectual and spiritual currents that came to dominate Western culture. Thus the arts, media, academe and not-for-profit foundations were easily transformed into counter-cultural ideological forces.

In those important sectors of modern American life, more sophisticated, politically correct, professionals control key gateways to power and influence where few Tea Party activists can tread. In the long term, therefore, unless a new and forceful intellectual Conservative Rebellion can grow in influence in those critical areas of cultural life, neither the Tea Party, the Republican Party, nor traditional conservatives can expect to prevail. The immediate and long term future that lies before us can be seen in the persons and policies of the Obama administration.

A forceful Conservative Rebellion requires philosophers, knowledgeable political leaders, non-ideological publications, wealthy benefactors and supportive institutions. The many "independent scholars" whose essays, articles, books and blogs make interesting reading are "independent" because American colleges and universities are hostile to their ideas. A revival of conservative ideas cannot occur if the influence of conservative intellectuals who create those ideas are denied careers suitable to their talents. The total domination of our Humanities and Social Science Departments by the Left—what James Piereson calls "The Left University"—places the future of the Conservative Rebellion in serious doubt.

To some extent, if our Rebellion becomes a conservative rout, that future rout could have been predicted for the many reasons that the administration of Ronald Reagan was called the "Reagan Revolution." Conservatives engage in rebellions, not revolutions, thus those who called Ronald Reagan's presidency a "revolution" did not fully appreciate the transitional character of his administration and the weakening influence of Conservative Rebels.

President Reagan was a very old man when elected in 1980 and he represented a generation much older than the young conservatives who clamored to join his administration. World War II, "D Day," the successful defeat of Nazi Germany, were remembered and celebrated by Reagan and his men. The young conservatives who had fought for Barry Goldwater and felt the sting of defeat by Lyndon Johnson were ignored. With the exception of Newt Gingrich, few members of the post-World War II generation would succeed in practical politics to the degree that success embraced Ronald Reagan. Only in 1994 did the post-World War II generation achieve some semblance of political power in the United States, but by then America had been transformed by the domination of the Left in all other sectors of American society and culture.

Thus we might despair.

Despair is an easy attitude to acquire. However, the policies of the Left will fail and future opportunities will come to enable principled conservatives to appeal to an electorate that may dimly remember the freedoms all Americans once enjoyed. Many younger conservative politicians have learned, or are now learning, the ropes of American politics and many more are in the pipeline. One or more of them may succeed where others failed.

But, if we forget the greater context of loss of a common civilization of the West and fail to engage in efforts to recover it, a dark night of despotism looms on the horizon and our children and grandchildren will be conditioned to accept a loss of freedom that a secular administrative state demands.

But, what is it that we must we recover from?

Injuries from external sources and internal ones inflicted on ourselves must be overcome, if the process of recovery is to begin. The effects of wars over the past one hundred years, and being mindful of the effect of our own Civil War of nineteenth-century America, must be included in the assessment of external injuries, as well as the absence of a philosopher of world class rank who captures our attention to the exclusion of contemporary ideologies on the right and left.

Let us begin first, however, with a review of external sources of injury. That greatest external source of injury is the many wars that were the consequences of Woodrow Wilson's intervention in World War I.

Thomas Fleming, editor of Chronicles of Culture, writes in an essay titled "The Wasted Century,"[20] that what was lost as a result of World War I was "a common civilization that developed out

20 Thomas Fleming, "The Wasted Century," Chronicles of Culture, June 2, 2014.

of the ruins of the Christianized Roman Empire." Woodrow Wilson's political religion exacerbated that conflict by injecting the United States into a war that was not in the national interest. At this distance, few alive today can report on the effects on American combatants from their service in the First World War, but Fleming's essay recalls the reflections of T. S. Eliot on the "unspeakable tragedies" of sixteen million dead and eighteen million wounded. All American military-related deaths totaled 117,000. Many of us, however, do remember the World War II generation and that they did not speak willingly of their experience. What we learned from them we had to drag out of them.

Living with war has become so common since World War I that we forget how an unbroken string of wars occasioned by the rise of totalitarian movements in Germany, Russia, China, Korea, Vietnam, and Cambodia, had conditioned Americans to accept military actions ordered by American presidents.

Finally, close to seventy years later and after too many military engagements, American citizens have become "war weary." But, the main effect of these wars, apart from the growth of the administrative state and the militarization of our intelligence services, was to distract our attention from the coarsening of American culture and the decline of American standards of civility that we inherited from an age before a Western *Christianitas* came to be abandoned.

Indeed, since World War II we have seen the decline of every institution of American civil society and, except for modern science and communications, we find ourselves in what may only be called "an historical trough," an era of decline, where we endure bad religion,[21] bad education, bad politicians, bad culture and, unfortunately, bad conservatism.

There is yet another voice to add, therefore, to the five other claimants to leadership of the Conservative Rebellion. I trace the origins of that voice to Fr. Stanley Parry's *Modern Age* essay on

---

21 See Ross Douthat, *Bad Religion. How We Became A Nation of Heretics* (New York: Free Press, 2012).

tradition in 1961, previously cited in Chapter 3, his Philadelphia Society presentation in February 1965 and to the writings of Gerhart Niemeyer. In Chapter 3, I promised to return to Niemeyer's final arguments in *Between Nothingness and Paradise* published in 1971.

My story of *The Conservative Rebellion* began with the observation that "over time, the American people have come to understand their nationhood as the mystical substance of their common existence. How this paradigmatic reality of the life of a nation is articulated shapes the American nation for action in history."

Niemeyer's discussion of this reality begins in the observation that a bond between political order and the order of being has been a casualty of "ideology."

What is this bond that has been lost?

For that we must discover the meaning of the historical continuity of society.

What is it in society that continues?

Unlike human beings, a society does not by its nature have a personal memory. By analogy, Niemeyer writes, a society has a remembered past by reference to "a present unity of action" that is like the identity of a person. ". . . [T]he past alone is what could give identity to a society."[22] The anthropological principle, "society is man writ large," moves us closer to understanding this aspect of society because we infer from our experience of our own existence that society exists also. But unlike man, society is "created." At the start, a society has no past, but over time the materials of an historical past can be created into a consciousness of an historical past.

An example that Niemeyer uses is that of ancient Israel.

> The fact is that the escapees from Egypt, when they finally stood in safety and freedom, experienced their deliverance as an act of God, an irruption of divine might into time and the affairs of men.[23]

22 Gerhart Niemeyer, *Between Nothingness and Paradise*, p. 145.
23 Ibid., p. 155.

How different was this experience of Israel's God from the gods of the other peoples of the ancient Near East?

Because the civilization of the West has been shaped by faith in revelation of God's intervention in history, it is very difficult for us to understand the radical break from the manner of interpreting experience by reference to cosmological gods. We simply do not interpret our experience of existence or nature by reference to cosmological gods. The moon, the sun, the wind, rain, thunder, lightning are, for us, physical phenomena, not gods. Yet for millennia the gods of the cosmos shaped ancient man's understanding of the sacred and the profane and explained the origin of the world and of empires. Ancient Israel, however, interpreted its existence by remembering a one-time intervention by God in history.

> A cosmological myth can be celebrated by reenacting again and again the story it relates. But an event that happened once in time and place, "before our eyes," even though experienced as a theophany, cannot be repeated or reenacted. God acted one time and his action can be only remembered.[24]

Niemeyer writes that "Once the Exodus theophany had grown into the order of a people living under God on the strength of their public past, history had become a mold of human existence, as such novel not only for 'Jacob and his son' but for the entire human race."[25]

History—our consciousness of time past, time present and time future—became a condition of Western human existence, and in the continuity of this society in history, Niemeyer sees, following Boethius, that "man in face of temporal mutation seeks to 'imitate the ever present immutability of (God's) life. . . .'"

From this perspective our nationhood as citizens of the United States is a mystic participation in divine reality that,

24   Ibid., p. 160.
25   Ibid., p. 162.

Niemeyer writes, "hinges on the all-important experience of a past at which a meeting occurred between time and eternity." Consciousness of that history shapes our understanding of the life of the American nation, an identity that imitates, again following Boethius, "'the ever simultaneous present immutability of God's life.'"[26] This reality, Niemeyer explains, can only be explained by myth.

Though it may seem improbable that the identity of modern America is shaped by myths, Niemeyer lists a number of truths we Americans affirm that are essentially mythic. Some uniquely American myths include the belief that individuals have souls; we proclaim an essential personal dignity and independence of mind. We distinguish time from eternity, and we attribute authority to "the people," and to the "law." We affirm an enduring Constitution, and that we as a nation exist "under God."[27] These myths do not depend on the consent of every American to their truth. Niemeyer suggests that the carriers of the truths of our myths may even be concentrated in a "remnant."[28]

Aristotle's analysis of the soul into rational and irrational parts is also foundational to Western man since something similar to revelation of Yahweh occurred in ancient Greece and led to rejection of the cosmological gods in the wake of a new truth about God in the discoveries of the Greek natural philosophers. That enabled Plato and Aristotle to differentiate the human psyche as the source of participation in divine reality.

Nous, Aristotle observes in his great *Nicomachean Ethics,* is the highest part and is "divine or the most divine thing in us." Through our *nous* we participate in the divine ground and our lives and actions are shaped by that experience. The irrational or concupiscent aspects of the soul are equally real, thus there are two tensions in the human soul: that of soul's rational part and "man's opaque psychic forces."

26   Ibid., p. 178.
27   Ibid., p. 191.
28   Ibid., p. 193.

They are not capable of lending life the transparency that characterizes the *noetic* consciousness, but Aristotle reminds us that they are capable of heeding the *nous* or refusing to heed it.[29]

This recalls what Aristotle explained about right by nature.

What is right can be known by mature men,[30] he said, but often we know it by reference to someone who knows what is right. In life we often ask ourselves, "What would he do?" That he or she may be someone we knew who could be relied upon for good advice. That is a powerful force in our private and in our public lives. These are persons who guide others in ways that can be political, or moral, or simply "just." The reality of their presence in our lives is celebrated in art, literature and motion pictures. Education from the elementary to secondary through college should aim to grow good character and replenish the numbers of mature men and women in each generation.

Niemeyer takes this essentially Aristotelian formulation and sharpens it with the assertion that

> Christianity is the center of our culture, the truth that has shaped our past and is still shaping our present, regardless of what the attitude of particular persons to it may be. We cannot realistically step out of this truth into "another one," we cannot in truth become Hindus or Buddhists, and least of all can an amalgam be made of all religions as a dwelling place for anybody. Western civilization came into existence through the unifying impulse of Latin Christianity. No other religion has ever

29   Ibid., p. 185.
30   Aristotle, *Nicomachean Ethics*, Martin Ostwald trans. (Indianapolis: Bobbs-Merrill, 1962). "Thus, what is good and pleasant differs with different characteristics or conditions, and perhaps the chief distinction of a man of high moral standards is his ability to see the truth in each particular moral question, since he is, as it were, the standard and measure for such questions." 1113a24. See also 1166a10, 1176a15 and 1176b20.

wielded a similarly powerful influence in the centuries of our cultural identity. The historical metamorphoses of our culture can be understood only in their relations to the Christian origins, even where these metamorphoses have not worked for but rather against Christianity.[31]

At this late stage in the decline of the West, it is unlikely that the Western Christianitas can be recovered. There is no modern Clovis to convert to Christianity and the ancient tribes of Western Europe have consolidated into modern nation states. In America the Bill of Rights included a provision that prohibited an establishment of religion. Though that restriction originally applied only to the national government, no states after 1818 maintained a church establishment. And no modern "Great Awakening" is likely to occur, nor have lasting consequences were it to occur. And though Stanley Parry believed that we conservatives have yet to find our own Plato or St. Augustine to whom we may repair for guidance, we should not overlook the presence of *daimonic*, mature men and women, who are carriers of the truth of Christianity and classical philosophy who daily contend against the corrosion of civil society by ideological movements. Eric Voegelin writes, "The new man who lives in the tension of the erotic tension toward his ground of being Plato calls the *daimonios aner*, i.e., a man who exists consciously in the tension of the in-between (*metaxy*), in which the divine and the human mutually partake of each other."[32] Aristotle's equivalent for the *daimonios aner* is the *spoudaios*, sometimes translated mature man.[33] Christian theology speaks of the reality of living in a State of Grace.

Those among us who are responsive to the *daimonic* aspect of our souls call us to a higher standard and share with us the hu-

---

31 Gerhart Niemeyer, "Christian Studies and the Liberal Arts College," in *The Loss and Recovery of Truth*, p. 511.

32 Eric Voegelin, "What is Political Reality?" in *Anamnesis*, p. 352.

33 Aristotle, *Nicomachean Ethics*, 1094a 19–26.

mility that comes from understanding that a higher aspect of our humanity is shaped by the transcendent God. These men and women are the true heroic conservatives and nurturing them is essential for renewal, for reducing the influence of political religion on American life and our recovery from centuries of decline.

At the end of the twenty-first century, will there be a vibrant, powerful, and spiritually healthy American nation? Will we even remember the civilization of the Christian West? Or will we suffer a loss of history and learn to accept bad economics, bad religion, failure in American foreign policy and the uncertainty of a world of forces seeking to destroy our country? The outcome is in the hands of new generations of Conservative Rebels and whether they can keep the Conservative Rebellion alive.

Index